RAILWAYS OF THE CARIBBEAN

David C. Rollinson

CARIBBEAN

First published 2001 by
MACMILLAN EDUCATION LTD
London and Oxford
Companies and representatives throughout the world

www.macmillan-caribbean.com

ISBN 0-333-73042-9

10   9   8   7   6   5   4   3   2   1
10 09 08 07 06 05 04 03 02 01

This book is printed on paper suitable for recycling and
made from fully managed and sustained forest sources.

Colour separation by Tenon & Polert Colour Scanning Ltd

Printed in Malaysia

A catalogue record of this book is available from the
British Library.

Maps by Richard Morris

Designed by Jeffrey Tabberner

Cover design by Stafford and Stafford

Typeset by Holbrook Design (Oxford) Limited

Dedicated to the railway men and women of the Caribbean.
Past, present and future.

Foreword

The Caribbean idyll is the silver sand beach, fringed with palm trees, with the transparent blue sea lapping gently at its edge. That is an experience that I and many visitors have enjoyed across the islands. If you live in the Caribbean, however, you will know of the great diversity in the size and nature of the islands: big and small, mountainous and flat reef, zephyr breezes and hurricane winds, calm tranquillity and rumbling volcanoes. You will know that this diversity is echoed in the racial and cultural mix of the Caribbean with its African, American and European history and its exciting blend of languages, politics and music.

Reflecting this diversity, David Rollinson has produced, in his *Railways of the Caribbean*, a first and excellent summary of the style and history of railways in the Caribbean. This describes the differences of engineering, construction and operation that vary with the terrain, history and overseas influence existing throughout the area.

Today we tend to view the Caribbean mainly as a leisure area, with its dominant industry that of tourism. But it has not always been so, especially in the eighteenth and nineteenth centuries when sugar was king. Then transport was slow and expensive, being by mule cart or sailing sloop, and the entrepreneurs of the day were quick to see the benefits of the new railways. In 1837 Cuba was the seventh country in the world to build a steam-powered railway. This was before Spain and only eight years after the Rainhill trials on the Liverpool and Manchester Railways in England. Jamaica followed in 1843 and Trinidad in 1864, by which time Cuba had over 700 miles of railway lines. While the peak of railway building, as elsewhere, was in the last quarter of the nineteenth century, the Caribbean was not a backwater of railway development. Van Horne, who led the Canadian Pacific across the Rockies, was then turning his attention to building a central line in Cuba, and railways were developed on the smaller islands right through to 1924. There were early experiments with diesel and electric power, some of which still survive in operation.

The overseas influences are clearly visible in the railway stock: Trinidad's railways showed British Colonial influence tempered by the effect of the Land-Lease Agreement with the United States during the Second World War. Guadeloupe was most definitely French, and Cuba showed an almost completely American influence until Castro's revolution.

That revolution and the following United States trade blockades put Cuba's railways, and much else in Cuba, into a time warp and the resultant mix of venerable steam and electric locomotives of the 1930s and 1940s plus Soviet and Eastern bloc diesels, has made Cuba a Mecca for railway enthusiasts all over the world. However, time is running out now that the lifting of the blockade and the reintroduction of Cuba to the Western world appears possible, leading inevitably to the modernisation and rationalisation of the transport fleet. Already second-hand locomotives and railcars have arrived from Canada and Spain. So if you want to see vintage Caribbean railways, go now.

Given the emphasis on tourism in the region, it is surprising that no one has made a real go of a tourist train similar to those in Europe, Japan and elsewhere. The Bermuda Railway was built for that purpose and both Antigua and St Kitts have had recent rather half-hearted attempts and might possibly, with a lot of restoration, try again. The small islands are more suited to that sort of enterprise but Puerto Rico is the only one with an active 'Tren del Sur'.

Various pictures stand out in my experiences of railways in the Caribbean. Like David Rollinson, my first introduction to the St Kitts railway was on the road from the airport. My attention was taken by the rear view of a very large bulldozer serenely moving without a driver through the sugar cane. On further investigations and a different angle I saw a diminutive diesel locomotive hidden from view hauling the monster on a bogie flat truck. It was outside the harvest season and after a very pleasant reception at the railway office, I was told that a maintenance train was out on the line if I cared to search for it. A third of the way around the island, I found the train stopped for lunch with the engine driver sitting in the shade of a large tree, reading the Scriptures from a large pulpit Bible.

The railways of Caroni Ltd, the national sugar company of Trinidad, were quite sophisticated in the last quarter of the twentieth century, with 24-hour radio-controlled operations during the harvest or 'Campaign'. One evening I was enjoying the extended hospitality of the traffic manager and an evening meal, when information came through that locals were collecting firewood by sawing up the sleepers on one of the open framework bridges. The night train of loaded cane was on its way down the line.

What followed was worthy of the movies, as our party leapt into a Land Rover and sped off towards the bridge in order to reach it before the train. As we drove down the last two miles of the permanent way, searchlights blazing, my dinner was well and truly shaken down!

The Sainte Madelaine Usine of Caroni dieselised its railways in 1956. A conservative management stored five locomotives, including two of its fine 2-6-2 Tanks in a siding about half a mile from its factory, just in case the diesels failed to cope. In 1970 they were still there, saplings and bushes growing around and through them and bees and snakes living inside. In the 1980s trees had grown up which today probably make up a dense but peculiar wood!

I have usually met with much courtesy from those on the mechanical and operational side of Caribbean railways. Often they are the same style of craftsmen who have kept things going in industries such as agriculture and mining. The building and operation of the railways brought a lot of the mechanical skills to the Caribbean and the need for a stable society to have these skills is paramount.

I felt very privileged to be asked by David Rollinson to write the foreword to this book which is not only a very enjoyable read for both the Caribbean visitor as well as the convinced railway enthusiast, but is also a valuable contribution to the history source books for the region. It will become a major reference work and I hope will be a spur to many readers to research further into the subject, either from the technical or the socio-economic viewpoint.

For those who enjoy the fascination of discovering history there is a lot of scope for detailed work, such as finding working railways that you did not know were still working, old artefacts and historical documents. With many of the railway companies being controlled or influenced from overseas, you don't necessarily need to live in the Caribbean to follow your particular favourite island's history. A colleague returning to Canada moved house, buying an old brownstone house in Toronto. In an ancient trunk left in the loft were a dozen full plate photographs of the Spanish American Ironstone Railway, taken at the turn of the last century. 'Buried Treasure' can be really rewarding! I am pleased to recommend this attractive and thoroughly researched book to all who love the Caribbean and who love railways, as a starting point for a journey into history, or as a souvenir of an exciting region.

Meanwhile, if you have not yet visited the remaining railways in the Caribbean, go now and take this book with you!

Roger Darsley

ROGER DARSLEY, M.Sc; Ch.P; M.Inst.P; FIFST
Railway Historian and Author

Acknowledgements

This book would not have been possible without the generous and knowledgeable help of Roger Darsley and Geoffrey Hill. The Caribbean locomotive lists of Allan de Koningh were of invaluable help.

The contributions, help and encouragement of the following are appreciated:Heiko Ahlers, Gerry Aird, Joan Albury (Bahamas Historical Society), Simmone Alleyne (Barbados National Trust), Luis Alvila (Belize Archives Dept), Larry Armony (Brimstone Hill Fortress National Park Society), William Ashley, Joan Bloom, Rosemary Bradley, Dr Jonathan Brown (Rural History Centre, University of Reading), Alan Burgess (Narrow Gauge Railway Society), Carol Burns, Paul Catchpole, Keith W. Clingan, Jenni O'Connor (Barbados National Trust), Bob Conrich, William Cornwall Jnr., Robert Devaux, Gail Dore (Nevis Historical and Conservation Society), Anita Ebanks (Cayman Islands National Museum), Mrs Eppie D. Edwards (National Library of Jamaica), Graham Fairhurst, Nancy Fisk (St Croix Landmarks Society), B. H. Friesen, Haluk Gurer, Kathryn Harmon, Lornette Hanley (Nevis Historical and Conservation Society), David Hayes, Margaret Kieckhefer (Library of Congress), Dr Peter Lee and Lawson Little (Narrow Gauge Railway Society), Doug Luery, Desmond Nicholson (Museum of Antigua and Barbuda), F. L. Pugh (Industrial Railway Society), Ruben A. Ramkissoon, S. C. Robinson (Industrial Railway Society), Rabbi Walter L. Rothschild, Dr Gail Saunders (Bahamas Archives), Betty Shannon (Barabados Museum and Historical Society), Mrs Stratmann, I. H. Thomas (Industrial Railway Society), John Powell, Brian Kershaw, Daru C. Rooke (The Leeds Industrial Museum), Sn. Diogenes Uceda (Falconbridge Dominicana, C. por A.), Carol Wakefield (St Croix Landmarks Society), Elizabeth Williams (The Jamaica Archives and Records Dept), David Winters, Gordon Wiseman and Richard Yudin.

Lastly and most importantly, my thanks to my wife Nancy, whose map-reading skills guided us through many Caribbean backroads in our search for the remnants of Caribbean railways, whose un-erring eye for smoke on the horizon in Cuba found locomotives and whose support has seen this project through to the end.

Preface

This book has its beginnings in a late departure from the airport in the Caribbean island of St Kitts in the mid-1980s. Our mid-afternoon flight to Canada was delayed by several hours, and being somewhat old Caribbean hands by then, my wife and I, forgoing the expensive and crowded airport snack bar, went into the airport car park to buy a cold beer and some fried chicken from the back of a pickup truck. Our temporary seat under a shady tree looked out over the St Kitts sugar factory railway marshalling yards, and it was not long before the late afternoon cane train trundled into view, its little red diesel locomotive working the train through the yard with a low throaty exhaust. It was a captivating scene.

After a number of years living and travelling in the Caribbean I began to realise that there was far more railway history in the region than I had expected, but this history was not in a form that a visitor to the region, or anyone interested in railways, could easily access. Hence this book.

No attempt has been made to produce a comprehensive history of the many public and private railways of the Caribbean; the book does not list in detail the locomotives and rolling stock that have passed through the hands of these railways. Nor does it relate every intimate detail of the thrust and parry of the political, financial and legal shenanigans that often seemed to have accompanied the building and operating of Caribbean railways. But, hopefully, the flavour and individuality of each railway has been captured, because each railway was as individual as the island in which it ran.

Research for this book spanned the Caribbean, North and South America, Great Britain and Europe, utilising material written in the five languages that are, or were, at one time used in the Caribbean. Wherever possible I have used photographs that I felt would make a contribution to the value of the book, even though in some instances these photographs may not be of the best quality. As reproduction resources on many Caribbean islands are usually not very sophisticated, and archives are not as well endowed with staff and financial resources as one would wish, in a number of cases I was just happy to be able to get a photograph!

Railways played an integral part in the development of the Caribbean islands and the Caribbean people, and as such need to be recognised for their contribution. I hope this book will provide some impetus for others to continue the work, before it is too late. For while a surprising amount of railway activity continues in the Caribbean, closure of the remaining systems continues. In the course of working on this book, the last railway in Trinidad closed, replaced by road transport, and in Cuba, the last bastion of steam railways, contractions in the sugar harvest and the economic deprivations caused by the continuing American trade embargo continue to affect the country's railways. Now is the time to travel if you want to enjoy the remaining Caribbean railways!

David Rollinson
NEVIS, WEST INDIES, 1999

Contents

▶ *In its smart red and yellow livery, a type TEM-2TK USSR – supplied Brynansk diesel locomotive and train heads through the yard on the outskirts of Matanzas, May 1998. (Author's collection)*

Chapter 1

Introduction

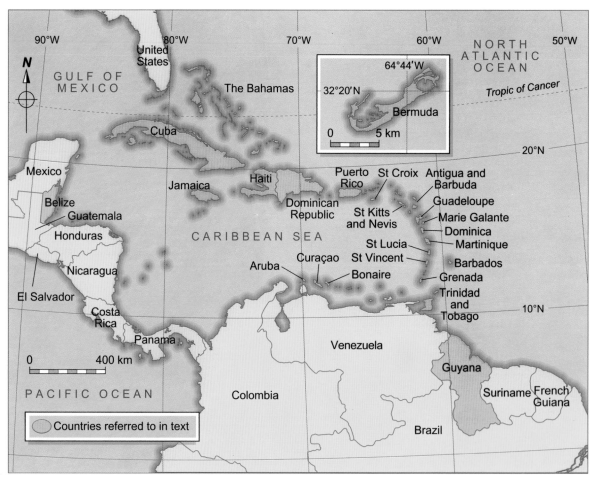

Honours for being the first operating Caribbean railway go to the 17-mile Havana to Bejucal line in Cuba, opened in 1837, only 12 short years after the momentous 1825 opening of the steam-powered Stockton and Darlington Railway in England. While the islands of the Caribbean might seem unlikely participants in the railway boom, a brief study of the history, politics and commerce of the region reveals a situation that was ripe for their introduction.

An 1800-mile-long chain of volcanic, sedimentary or limestone land masses of varying sizes, the Caribbean islands extend from the Bahamas, just off the coast of Florida in the north to the southern-most island of Trinidad, off the coast of Venezuela. Caribbean islands come in all shapes and sizes. Cuba, the largest of the chain has a landscape composed of flat fertile plains, cool green mountains and hundreds of miles of sandy beaches, with a population of over 11 million, while the tiny, 5-square-mile Dutch island of Saba in the northern Leewards has virtually no beach and a population of about 1200 souls living in small settlements perched precariously on the sheer sides of an extinct volcanic peak. Between these two extremes is a mix of topography and climate that has supported human settlement for over 2000 years and produced everything from sugar and bananas to gold and oil.

While forming part of the American continent, the former colonies of British Guiana and British Honduras, now the independent countries of Guyana and Belize, continue to remain politically, socially and economically affiliated with the islands of the Caribbean. Bermuda, while far to the north of the Caribbean, shares a colonial history similar to that found in most English-speaking Caribbean islands and continues to have extensive cultural ties with many of the islands.

The 'New World' islands of the Caribbean were the scene of rapid colonialisation by Spain, Holland, England, France, Denmark and Sweden, beginning in the early decades of the seventeenth century. However, the islands were of relatively little commercial consequence until the introduction of sugar cane into the region in the mid-1600s. Cuba, colonised by the Spanish in 1512, had entered the sugar industry in a small way by the year 1590 with some *estancias*, the small estates of the island, growing and processing cane on a limited basis. But tobacco and cotton constituted the main crops in Cuba and on the English islands until the beginning of the sugar era, which most probably started in Barbados in 1644. At this time James Drax, a substantial plantation owner growing mainly cotton and tobacco, made sufficient

Torrential rains in the Caribbean made travel over even the shortest distances dangerous and inconvenient. The transportation of large amounts of sugar in conditions such as this was impossible. (Royal Commonwealth Society Collection, Cambridge University Library)

sugar to be able to afford the purchase of 34 slaves from the proceeds. Six years later, Barbados had raised its export revenues to £3 million sterling, an astronomical sum for the time, and one almost solely based on sugar.

By the mid-1700s over a dozen islands in the Caribbean were growing sugar cane. Enormous fortunes were to be made producing sugar, at the time a luxury food with the same status as coffee, cocoa and tea. By the 1750s Muscavado, the coarse lump sugar made on all the islands, sold in Jamaica for 33 shillings and eight pence per pound or over £3000 sterling per ton!

In Cuba the coming of the railway was precipitated by the need to transport large amounts of raw sugar and molasses, a by-product of sugar making, to the coast for export by sea. As the Cuban sugar industry expanded further inland away from the coastline and traditional centres of agriculture, road improvement became an economic necessity. The damaging effects of tropical rains could be minimised by laying cobbled roads, often using local field stone. During the 1700s many narrow bridle paths were converted to year-round public roads able to handle ox carts, the carts replacing the large number of pack animals used previously. Eventually, even carts were unable to

The transportation requirements for even a small sugar mill is evident in this late 1800s view of a small Cuban steam-powered sugar factory. (St Croix Landmarks Society Research Library)

◀ *Waiting for the train, probably in Trinidad. The coming of the railway, with fares low enough for working people, brought about major social and political changes in the Caribbean. (Royal Commonwealth Society Collection, Cambridge University Library)*

▼ *A large new sugar Central in Matanzas Province, Cuba, in the early 1900s, complete with railway and large capacity sugar cane wagons. (Author's collection)*

transport the growing volumes of sugar and molasses to the docks, and railways were resorted to in order to carry out this task in a timely way. It is now generally accepted that in Cuba it was the coming of the railway, not the introduction of steam-powered sugar mills, that produced the massive and swift expansion of that country's sugar industry in the mid-1800s.

On other islands, post-emancipation changes in island populations and settlement patterns (the development of large urban centres) stimulated a need for mass transit, one that was an improvement over the traditional overland or sea routes. Public railways in the Caribbean, either Government or privately owned, were developed to meet the needs of this changing society. Whilst not all of the railways were successful, they played an important role by contributing to the social and economic development taking place during the post-emancipation and late-colonial era of the Caribbean. Lumbering, mining, oil refining, bananas

7001. Sugar Mill, Cuba.

Animal power on Caribbean railways was quickly replaced by locomotives, but ox-power could be usefully employed moving cane cars within the factory confines, as shown in this c.1930 photograph probably taken at Woodford Lodge factory in Trinidad. (Author's collection)

and tourism all benefited from and encouraged the development of public railroads in the region.

The industrialisation of the sugar industry on many of the larger Caribbean islands in the late 1800s and early 1900s precipitated a second railway-building boom. Early Caribbean sugar estates were small in size, 100 acres being considered large on most islands in the early eighteenth century. The cane mills and sugar boiling walls attached to each of these small estates were within easy reach of the most distant fields. However, the large Central factories, introduced in the late 1880s in response to the declining world price of sugar, had an appetite for cane well beyond the ability of local fields to satisfy, and cane had to be hauled from fields often at a distance where it was uneconomic to use traditional wheeled transport. It

was at this juncture that sugar cane railways became an integral and essential part of the Caribbean landscape on islands large and small.

While not widely dispersed in the Caribbean, minerals are found on a number of islands and the development of mineral railways, often the quintessential industrial railway, developed on a number of islands. Iron ore, bauxite, phosphate, manganese and gold have all been carried by locomotive-hauled trains in the Caribbean. Today not only does this form of transport continue, but several extensive non-locomotive railways continue to move minerals within the region.

It would seem that in the early years of the twentieth century, any self-respecting town or city could boast a street railway. Urban areas throughout the Caribbean expanded in the early 1900s as a result of the mass movement of people from the post-emancipation agricultural countryside to urban centres of industry and commerce. Soon these urban centres had extensive street railway systems, initially often animal powered but later converted to use electricity from steam- or water-powered generating stations that were being built for lighting and industrial power.

Most Caribbean railways are now but a memory, the victims of road transport and changes in the local economy. However, in Cuba almost 5000 miles of rail line continue to provide an inexpensive, and essential, means of passenger transportation, and vintage narrow and standard gauge steam locomotives continue to haul trains of cane cars to the mills. In Jamaica it is still possible to see massive North American-built diesel locomotives hauling ore cars through a lush tropical landscape and in Haiti and the Dominican Republic there is some railway activity during the winter cane harvest. Further south in St Kitts a stable of smartly turned out narrow gauge diesel locomotives haul precarious trains of four-wheel cane cars from around the island to the central processing factory near the airport. In Puerto Rico, once the home of a substantial railway system, the spirit is kept alive by a short tourist railway that provides fun and nostalgia each weekend for both locals and visitors, and a new urban rail system being built in San Juan.

The development of suburban areas around the major cities in the Caribbean was often encouraged by the introduction of a street railway. In this early 1900s photograph the Hope Gardens car waits for passengers to board, before heading back down town. Hope Gardens is now part of the Kingston urban conurbation. (Jamaica National Library)

Chapter 2

Caribbean railway operations

Railway operations in the Caribbean showed a remarkable versatility and diversity, considering the small size of most of the systems and their relative isolation. An unpredictable climate, local and international politics, combined with fluctuating economic fortunes often made railway operations in the Caribbean very difficult. However, railway staff and railway owners persisted, often through great hardship, to run as effective a service as they could under the prevailing conditions; a tradition being continued in Cuba today.

Caribbean railways adopted a wide range of gauges, usually for single-line operation. Permanent ways varied from the highly engineered, standard gauge and express quality lines to very narrow gauge, hastily and inexpensively-laid tramways wending their way through cane fields. On these tracks a fascinating collection of locomotives powered by steam, gasoline, alcohol, diesel oil and electricity hauled everything from passengers to bananas in a variety of imported and home-made rolling stock.

Train control in most cases was basic. Many railways had no signalling equipment at all, while others used a system of telegraph and telephone, lanterns or flags. Only in later days did the more extensive systems use mechanically-operated semaphore signals, with automatic electric signals in areas of intensive working.

The permanent way

Constructing a railway permanent way in the Caribbean was often fraught with problems. The speculative nature of many of the railways often meant that money was in short supply for construction, with the protracted length of time taken for building often resulting in cost over-runs. Frequently the inaugural parts of the line had fallen into poor condition before the full extent of the line was in operation.

The lack of investment money sometimes led to the surveyor's route recommendations being ignored, to be replaced instead by the most direct, cheapest route. While providing short-term savings in construction costs, this tactic usually led to a track with sharp curves, unsuitable gradients and the adoption of expensive bridges and tunnels, all to the long-term financial detriment of the railway.

While many island railways could be laid through flat coastal areas, mountainous interiors posed considerable difficulties for builders. Tropical rainfall and mountainous terrain combined to provide civil engineers with challenges in the form of bridges over deep ravines that in the rainy season became swollen torrents, often of sufficient strength to undermine bridge piers and undercut ledges carrying the track. Tunnels were usually the only alternative to lengthy and costly detours. In Jamaica, where the main line ran through the central mountain district, a total of 41

tunnels, with a combined length of over 5000 feet, and five substantial viaducts and bridges had to be built. The island of Hispaniola shares many of the physical characteristics of central Jamaica, and the 715 ft-long steel deck bridge on the Ferrocarril Central Dominicano (one of the longest bridges on any Caribbean railway) presented a substantial engineering challenge at the time of its construction. Across the border in Haiti, the 109-mile-long Compagnie Nationales des Chemin de fer d'Haiti had over 20 substantial bridges along its length. The ill-fated Bermuda Railway was plagued during its whole operational life by the cost of maintaining the many bridges used due to their metal construction and proximity to the highly corrosive effects of sea water.

The final choice of route often dictated the use of some substantial grades, and the punishing 1 in 31 on the Barbados line and the numerous 1 in 50 gradients on the Bermuda Railway, were a continual challenge for drivers. The initial decision to use steep grades in order to keep line construction costs low, rather than take a longer, more gentle route, often resulted in higher operating costs for the railway and more work for train crews, especially where train loads were restricted. In Barbados, splitting the train into two sections had to be resorted to in order for light-weight narrow gauge locomotives to move trains up the grade by adhesion only. In some cases, as in the Dominican Republic, rack or geared locomotives had to be introduced on account of the steep grades used.

The cost of imported rail was a major expense for most Caribbean railways. On many systems light rail was used initially, but as service demands increased and heavier locomotives and trains were introduced, so rail weights increased. By the mid-1920s most of the Cuban public main lines had been upgraded to 80 lb per yard rail, with lighter 60 or 65 lb rail being used on branch lines and sidings. In Puerto Rico the metre

gauge main line used 40 lb to 60 lb rail with 30 lb rail often being used on the lighter, metre gauge cane railways. On smaller systems with light loads, rail as light as 12 lb per yard was used. New rail was an expense that was delayed as long as possible on many systems, especially towards the end of the railway's active life, with the inevitable result that the badly-worn rails contributed to mechanical damage to the engines and rolling stock, a slow and bumpy ride for the passengers and a full work schedule for the permanent way gangs.

The general use of wood sleepers on Caribbean railways led to a search for local timber that would be inexpensive, yet survive the depredations of weather and insects. Eventually experience taught what were the best species for local conditions, and many railways began to use local hardwoods exclusively, often harvested from their own lands, to replace expensive, imported, cypress sleepers. Locally procured sleepers

While the railway provided a more secure and comfortable way to travel, Mother Nature could still wreak havoc. Track damage on the Ewarton extension, Jamaica Railway, in 1886, the result of a tropical storm and subsequent land slide. (National Library of Jamaica)

9

A busy scene at the Batabano railway station, in Cuba, c.1898. Batabano was an important port on the south coast, and was connected to Havana by the Caminos de Hierro de La Habana. (St Croix Landmarks Society Research Library)

were expected to provide 10 to 15 years of service before requiring replacement. Steel sleepers were used on narrow gauge cane tramways or when portable lines were used in the fields, but high cost usually precluded their general use. The new urban light rail system being built in San Juan, Puerto Rico, and some of the refurbished Cuban main lines, now use concrete sleepers.

The choice of gauge

Track gauge in the Caribbean covered a wide range, from standard (4 ft 8½ in) to extreme narrow gauge (1 ft 11½ in). While standard gauge was adopted on common carrier lines in Bermuda, Cuba, Jamaica, Trinidad and Guyana, in Haiti, the Dominican Republic, Puerto Rico, Barbados and Belize narrow gauge was used. Subsequent experience on several of the standard gauge lines showed that the adoption of narrow gauge would have significantly reduced construction and operating costs, with the Barbados railway even reducing its original narrow gauge in an attempt to effect savings and improve operating efficiency.

A strong case could be made for the adoption of narrow gauge in the Caribbean. The initial 'battle of the gauges' in England had been between Stephenson's 4 ft 8½ in gauge and Brunel's 7 ft 0¼ in gauge. Even after the issue was resolved by legislation in 1846 in favour of Stephenson, it was well into the 1870s before it became commonly known as 'standard gauge'.

While standard gauge undoubtedly offered advantages where high speed and large hauling capacity were required, the use of narrow gauge had a number of financial and operating advantages that for railway building in the Caribbean were important considerations. Narrow gauge reduced the initial cost of track construction and the cost of locomotives and rolling stock, while some reduction in maintenance costs would be realised from the slower speeds and lighter train loads usually encountered on narrow gauge systems.

The opening of the narrow gauge Festiniog Railway in Wales had proved to be a turning point in the adoption of narrow gauge for common carrier railways and saw the beginning of a narrow gauge railway culture. Steam-powered railways were already being built to gauges less than standard in the early 1860s, with narrow gauge public railways operating in such diverse locations as Queensland (Australia) and Norway.

Railway building in the Caribbean reflected this growing confidence in narrow gauge lines, and as public and private railways were conceived and built throughout the region, many of them adopted a gauge less than standard. As speed of service was never a major consideration on the majority of Caribbean lines, whereas low operating costs were, the major objection to narrow gauge, the logistics of gauge break between two dissimilar connecting lines, was never an issue. In several islands, sugar factory lines were made the same gauge as the public railway, and rolling stock could be transferred directly from industrial line to main line with resulting efficiency and cost savings.

Portable railways

While several permanent railways in the Caribbean adopted a gauge of less than 24 inches, generally speaking this extreme narrow gauge was more often adopted for use on the portable tramway systems that became common on sugar plantations beginning in the late 1800s.

As sugar cane acreage expanded, the distance from the fields to the permanent re-load points on the factory railway became so great that the high cost and slow speed of this transfer became a major concern. But as cane fields were only harvested every two or three years, it was not economic to lay permanent rails. Two-wheel ox carts, the traditional method of field transport, became bogged down in wet conditions, while the light loads that the oxen could haul often made it difficult to supply the hungry new Central factories with sufficient cane to maintain a consistent crushing schedule. Evidently, an alternative method of field transport, one that was portable, not susceptible to soft ground and capable of moving large volumes of cane efficiently and economically had a large potential market.

The English engineering company of John Fowler had experience in the Caribbean sugar industry through supplying steam-powered ploughing and traction engines to large estates in islands such as

Extreme narrow gauge portable railways were used on sugar estates on a number of Caribbean islands. This delightful 20 in gauge locomotive and train was built by John Fowler & Co., of Leeds, England, in 1879. (Fowler Collection, Rural History Centre, University of Reading)

Cuba, so it was perhaps inevitable that they saw the potential for expanding into the portable railway market. The French company Decauville Aine was producing portable narrow gauge track sections, cars and locomotives by 1878, and at the Paris Exhibition in 1889 were able to exhibit a 60 cm (23 in) gauge railway, complete with locomotives and rolling stock. Many portable lines of this type were later supplied by Decauville to sugar estates in the French islands of Guadeloupe and Martinique.

In 1877 Fowlers obtained a licence to manufacture portable railway systems on the Decauville principle. By 1878 they had produced a 1 ft 10 in gauge portable system, with sections of light rail permanently fastened to corrugated iron sleepers and suitable for laying on soft, un-ballasted, ground. A small steam locomotive demonstrated the practicality of the system by hauling a three and a half ton load around a track laid to very tight curves. But it was the design of track that proved to be the key to the success of the system. Track sections, usually around 10 ft in length, were light enough to be lifted by two men, and the permanent fixing of the lightweight rails to the pressed metal sleepers prevented rail spread, the scourge of

traditionally laid track. In 1885 a Fowler Patented Portable Railway was in use in the cane fields of Cuba, and from this early success the company went on to develop a number of small patented steam locomotives, cane cars and passenger coaches especially for light railways and cane tramways.

Other manufacturers entered the market for portable track, with Robert Hudson Ltd., from England, becoming a major supplier of light railway equipment to the Caribbean, as was the German company, Arthur Koppel. Koppel had a representative in Cuba and a number of his systems were introduced to the island and Puerto Rico, beginning in the late 1800s.

Train control

Most Caribbean railways operated single track systems. Train control was never very sophisticated and generally speaking, the simpler the system adopted the better. Only as traffic volumes increased on some of the more substantial systems was more sophisticated mechanical and electrical signalling, (telegraph or telephone controlled), installed.

On many common carriers trains ran out to the furthest terminus (often at the end of the line) and then returned, so there was only ever one train on the track at any one time. On other railways trains travelled towards each other on the single track, crossing by means of passing loops that were usually situated at stations. In Cuba, as the main lines were expanded to double track a more complex control system was necessary at the larger terminals.

Hand signals, flags and lanterns usually sufficed on most lines, later to be supplemented with telegraph or telephone connections between stations. As trains were notoriously late, there could never be any certainty that the established passing locations would actually be adhered to, so station-to-station contact by telegraph or telephone helped. In Trinidad even this system was looked on with some suspicion at one time as the telephone and telegraph system used the same line for transmission. As the telephones had no bells fitted it was necessary to telegraph first to let someone know the telephone was about to be used. Apparently the confusion this caused rendered the system somewhat inadequate for train control purposes!

The Bermuda Railway, with its frequent service, used a key token for drivers to ensure safety, with the line being worked on a block system with possession of the key for that block allowing the train to proceed. Other lines used the telegraph block system, where access to blocks or sections of line was controlled by the passing of authority for the train to proceed by telegraph. This system often incorporated hand operated semaphores at junctions or in stations. In Jamaica the movement of trains within the limits of the busy Kingston station was controlled by a station pilot who had the only set of keys necessary to unlock and change points.

Cane railways and tramways seldom needed a signalling system, although in later years the introduction of basic telegraph networks and then two-way radios and a radio-equipped central control, as used today on St Kitts, significantly improved train control and efficiency.

On most islands road and rail traffic was light enough that crossing gates were not needed. However, in heavily-populated islands crossing gates, manned by railway employees, were used at all main intersections of highway and railway. Given the slow speeds of most trains and the infrequent service, fatal crossing accidents seem to have been uncommon, but they have happened. A railway-crossing accident reported in Cuba in 1997 resulted in considerable loss of life.

Motive power and rolling stock

Caribbean railway owners displayed an eclectic taste when it came to the purchase of motive power and rolling stock. Locomotives as varied as the massive, American-built Mallets used on the American Railway of Puerto Rico, diminutive cane tramway tank engines, home-made rail cars and Soviet-built diesel locomotives have all polished rails in the region over the years.

Purpose-built railway cars were quite common on Caribbean railways. The development of the banana industry in the region required the construction of special cars for this fragile fruit. The photograph shows two-purpose built banana cars of the British Honduras Railway loaded with green bananas ready for transportion to the pier and export to either England or North America. (Royal Commonwealth Society Collection, University of Cambridge Library)

▶ Habana, locomotive No.19 of the Caminos de Hierro de La Habana, was a high-stepping 4-4-0 built by Baldwin Locomotive Works in 1888. (Railroad Museum of Penna. (PHMC) H. L. Broadbelt collection)

▼ The Manati Sugar Company owned vast estates in Cuba. This 3 ft 0 in gauge Mallet was supplied to the company's extensive railway by Baldwin in 1917. (Railroad Museum of Penna. (PHNC) H.L. Boadbelt collection)

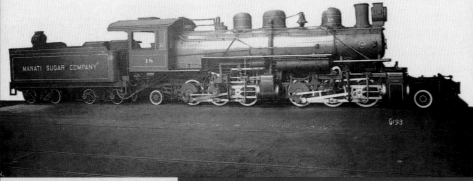

▶ Tank engines were used on many Caribbean railways. This little 2 ft 6 in gauge locomotive was supplied to the Spanish America Iron Co. of Cuba by Dickson Mfg. Co (later part of ALCO) in 1900. (ALCO Historic Photos)

While public railways in the Caribbean carried passengers and freight in a wide variety of rolling stock, enormous volumes of sugar cane were moved annually by private railways in specially-designed cane cars. The development of other agricultural crops in the region, especially bananas from the mid-1800s onwards, brought about the introduction of special cars for the transportation of this fragile fruit. The later development of the region's mining industries saw the introduction of another range of rolling stock.

Motive power

When the first railway in the Caribbean opened in November of 1837, the steam locomotives used were imported from England. They were replaced by American-built locomotives after a relatively short working life, a precursor to the long-running, but seemingly one-sided, battle between American, Canadian, British and European locomotive builders for a share of the lucrative Caribbean market.

While many Caribbean railways failed before they were able to make the transition from steam to internal combustion or electricity, modernisation did take place where running costs needed to be reduced or service improved. It remains a remarkable feature of the railways in Cuba today that century-old steam locomotives are working only a few miles away from electric rail cars built in the 1970s.

Caribbean railway managers were faced with a number of decisions when purchasing locomotives. In the inaugural phase of equipping a railway with locomotives, colonial loyalties exercised a tremendous influence, as was to be expected. The development of colonies was, in part, carried out in order to enhance trade 'at home' whenever possible. Early railways in former British colonies such as Barbados, British Guiana and Jamaica purchased locomotives made in

Great Britain, even though they were often replaced at a later date by the products of North American manufacturers. Caribbean railway companies were often owned or controlled by outside investors, more familiar with locomotives and railway operation in their own country, and the railway's buying agents were often located overseas. As many Cuban railways were owned by American interests, their motive power reflected this ownership with companies such as Baldwin, ALCO, Lima Locomotive Works, and Porter and Rogers supplying large numbers of locomotives. On larger islands such as Cuba, locomotive and rolling-stock manufacturers had resident agents, people who knew not only local conditions but no doubt were able to develop working relationships with railway managers and locomotive superintendents.

Whatever technical, financial or political constraints affected the purchase of motive power for Caribbean railways, they did not prevent the purchase of a wide range of motive power, including locomotives that at the time could be considered to be on the 'cutting edge' of technology. Operating considerations obviously played a substantial role in the decision to purchase a certain type of locomotive and track gauge. Line grades and curves determined wheelbase. Wheel configuration and hauling power was dependent on these factors as well as the type of service the railway was offering. No doubt the challenge was to match the motive power to the demands of the traffic and permanent way departments. Equally as important was the ability of the railway's workshops and mechanics to keep these locomotives operating.

Locomotive repair and maintenance was often the Achilles' heel of Caribbean railways. Those on the

The last steam locomotives used on many Caribbean railways were 2-8-0 tender types. This powerful, two-cylinder locomotive was supplied to the metre-gauge Fajardo Development Co. in Puerto Rico by ALCO in 1935. (ALCO Historic Photos)

smaller islands often lacked the technical resources, mechanical equipment and money to maintain even a small fleet in good mechanical condition. And while some of the larger lines had well-equipped workshops, reference is often made to the inadequacies of motive power depots. In Barbados in the 1920s the repair facilities were noted as being 'meagre' at best.

Many steam locomotive parts could be manufactured or rebuilt in the repair shop of the railways with fairly basic, yet robust, machine tools. In islands such as Cuba and the Dominican Republic, the skills needed to keep the steam-powered sugar factories running could also be turned to steam locomotive maintenance and repair. However, many railways did not have the advantages offered by well-equipped repair shops with adequate and trained staff, and as a consequence regular maintenance fell by the wayside and only emergency repairs were ever tackled. It was not unusual for a railway to have had a number of locomotives on its roster, with only one or two in workable condition.

If the business of the railway increased so did the size and power of locomotives used. American investment in Cuba and Puerto Rico, for example, led to a gradual improvement of the railway service. This was reflected in a massive renewal of main-line locomotive fleets, with modern, high-power and high-speed, locomotives replacing the old, worn out and under-powered. Locomotives with 2-6-0, 2-8-0 and 2-8-2 wheel arrangements seemed to be very popular, as even with their relatively light axle weights they could haul considerable loads and yet have a good turn of speed when needed. Larger, technically more complex, locomotives occasionally appeared in the Caribbean. Baldwin's first Mallet 2-6-6-2 tender locomotive went to a sugar railway in the Dominican Republic in the early 1900s, to be followed by others to Cuba and Puerto Rico. At almost the same time three

English-made 0-6 + 6-0 Kitson Meyer tank locomotives went to Jamaica for use on the island's public railway. It would be interesting to know if the additional mechanical complexity of these locomotives turned out to be worthwhile from an operational standpoint. A number of American geared locomotives were supplied to railways in the Dominican Republic and the Bahamas. While their slow speed provided some advantages, perhaps these were outweighed by their additional mechanical complexity.

Early Caribbean steam locomotives burned imported coal or locally-harvested wood. While vast quantities of bagasse, the dried crushed sugar cane residue from the cane mills, were used as a boiler fuel in the sugar factories where it could be handled by conveyor and automatic stoking furnaces, its bulk made it somewhat unsuitable for use as a locomotive fuel, although Bagnalls and Kerr Stuarts of England developed or supplied bagasse-fired locomotives. In the early days of the British Guiana Railway it was suggested that dried local peat would make a suitable locomotive fuel, but the idea was not taken further. A number of Caribbean railways converted to oil firing as oil supplies became more generally available and burner technology improved. While oil, like coal, was imported, it was much easier to handle than coal and oil storage tanks could be provided at strategic points along the line, often combined with watering stops. Today, in Cuba, locally-produced oil is still used by steam locomotives on the cane lines.

The Caribbean often experiences long dry periods, and sugar cane is notoriously flammable in these conditions. As both wood and coal are prone to produce sparks when used as a boiler fuel, many narrow gauge steam locomotives destined for use amongst cane fields were fitted with spark arresting chimneys.

The introduction of internal combustion engined locomotives brought advantages and disadvantages to Caribbean railways. The potential faster turn-round times and reduced maintenance requirements of diesel- and gasoline-powered locomotives promoted an increase in their use on both public and private railways during and immediately after the First World War. However, the change from steam was not all advantageous. Refined fuel was imported, expensive and subject to fluctuating supply. The maintenance and repairs needed by engines and transmissions were often more complex than those needed to keep a steam locomotive going, and the necessary skills were often in short supply. Replacement parts had to be purchased from overseas as they were usually too complex to be made in the repair shop, and their cost proved an embarrassment for railways in the latter days of their operation when they were virtually broke.

Large, main-line, diesels began to make their appearance in the Caribbean after the Second World War, with many still being in use today. In Cuba diesel locomotives from North America, Europe and the former Soviet block work on both the public and sugar factory lines, and in Jamaica English and North American-built diesel locomotives continue to haul bauxite trains.

Small, narrow gauge, diesel or gasoline locomotives found considerable use on cane railways, given the benefits of lower operating and maintenance costs. The first petrol-powered locomotives appeared on Caribbean sugar railways during, or just after, the First World War, when a number of ex-military, English-made Motor Rail locomotives found homes on cane railways in Antigua, St Kitts and Trinidad. The use of internal combustion-powered locomotives increased, and as the original steam locomotives came to the stage where they needed to be replaced in the late 1920s or early 1930s, diesel locomotives were usually

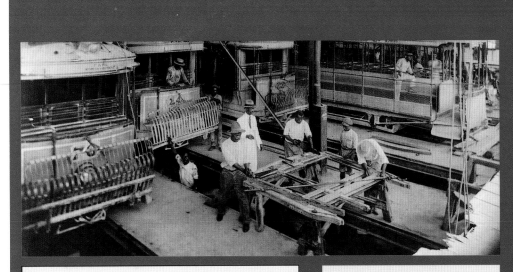

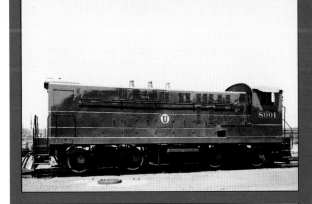

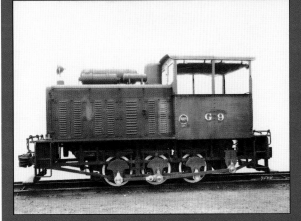

▲ The coming of railways to the Caribbean greatly helped in the introduction of new technology, skills and crafts to the region. This scene was recorded in the Kingston car barn of the West India Electric Co., some time between 1907 and 1923. (National Library of Jamaica)

◀ Internal combustion–engined locomotives were introduced into the Caribbean in the First World War period and quickly gained a foothold. This powerful main-line diesel locomotive was built for the United Railway of Havana by Baldwin in 1952. (Railroad Museum of Penna. (PHMC) H.L. Broadbelt collection)

◀ Internal combustion–engined locomotives also found favour on Caribbean industrial railways. The United Fruit Co. purchased this 3 ft. 0 inch gauge gas–engined locomotive from Baldwin in 1925 for use on its extensive estates in Cuba. (Railroad Museum of Penna. (PHMC) H.L. Broadbelt collection)

▶ *Electricity became available in a number of the larger Caribbean islands with the advent of steam or water-powered generating stations in the early 1900s. The Havana Central purchased standard gauge, steeple cab, electric locomotive No.1 in 1906 from ALCO. The locomotive was most likely used on the network of electric systems radiating out from Havana. (ALCO Historic Photos)*

▶ *Passenger accommodation on Caribbean railways ranged from the opulent on a number of Cuban railways to the very basic on many others. This 50-passenger bogie car was supplied by Fowlers of England in 1925 to the Port Mourant Plantation in Demerara (Guyana). The cars were supplied as metal work only and were assembled using local wood at the plantation. (Fowler Collection, Rural History Centre, University of Reading)*

Former steam locomotive suppliers to sugar estates, even the more conservative British manufacturers, became aggressive promoters of diesel-engined locomotives. English companies such as Fowler, Hunslet and Armstrong Whitworth had small 0-4-0 or 0-6-0 locos available by the early 1930s and Vulcan, Plymouth and Brookville became major American suppliers of diesel or gasoline locomotives to the Caribbean during the same period. Diesel mechanical, diesel hydraulic and diesel electric locomotives, many by the well-known English builder Ruston and Hornsby, were supplied to cane railways in the region and some continue to work today.

Electrically-powered locomotives have been a feature of Caribbean railways for many years. While not widespread, electric railways and urban street car services could be found on a number of the more populated and developed islands; in parts of Cuba industrial and passenger services continue to be provided by electric locomotives and electric rail cars. By 1914 electric locomotives were in operation in Puerto Rico and Cuba, their introduction linked to the development of electric power generation projects.

Rolling stock

Given the scope and variety of railway operations in the Caribbean, it is no surprise that a wide variety of rolling stock found its way into the region. From plush, standard gauge, American-style passenger cars, to rickety, narrow gauge, four-wheel trucks stacked high with sugar cane, the variety of rolling stock to be found in the Caribbean was as varied as the locomotives that hauled them.

Contemporary illustrations of the first passenger train in the Caribbean in 1837, between Havana and Bejucal, show open-sided four-wheel passenger cars being hauled by the line's inaugural locomotive. The

the replacement. Advertisements began appearing in the sugar industry trade press extolling the virtues of diesel locomotives over steam locomotives for sugar estate use at this time. Prominence was given to the lower running costs per mile for small diesel locomotives, estimated at being at least half of those of a steam locomotive, and their lower maintenance costs. The higher capital cost of these small diesel locomotives was estimated to be paid off in less than two years with the savings accrued from their lower operating costs.

cars resemble the basic passenger accommodation in use on railways in England and America at that time, but progress came quickly, and in 50 years contemporary photographs from Cuba show solidly-built, American-style, wood-bodied carriages mounted on bogie trucks. First-class accommodation on the Ferrocarril de Matanzas boasted an ornate interior with an abundance of carved wood and brass hardware, with individual seats facing inwards, no doubt the epitome of railroad travel in Cuba in the last years of the nineteenth century.

In comparison with this luxury, railway passengers in British Guiana at this time were transported in short wood-bodied carriages running on four wheels and fitted with what appears to be an open upper deck with a bench seat running the length of the carriage. Given the climate in the country, this must have been the third-class seating and passengers needed to be indifferent to the occasional soaking from a tropical downpour!

Passenger rail cars were adopted by a number of Caribbean railroads and usually provided a more substantial level of accommodation compared to the regular coaching stock. In Cuba, Mack rail cars ('why stop one hundred and fifty tons of steel to collect a thirty cent fare' was the Mack company's sales pitch) were tried, and in other islands rail car sets were imported from England. The interiors of the Bermuda Railway's Pullman cars were light and airy, with wicker chairs for passengers, a perfect combination for a railway offering a service as a tour train as much as a means of transport. The Metro-Cammell and Budd rail cars, supplied to Jamaica and Cuba respectively, would have provided a good level of passenger comfort, always important when speeds were slow and delays numerous.

While Cuba is the only country in the region currently to maintain a scheduled passenger service, it

has to be said that if recent personal experience is anything to go by, travel in one of the Cuban-built Taino passenger cars between Havana and Matanzas today is a far cry from the luxury once offered on this line! However, for the railway *aficionado*, it is a fascinating experience.

On islands such as Puerto Rico, Cuba, Barbados and Trinidad, revenue generated by the seasonal haulage of sugar cane made an important contribution to the public railway's finances. As this business evolved, so did the design of cane wagons. From the small, four-wheel, narrow gauge vehicles used on the cane tramways evolved massive, bogie-trucked, standard gauge cane cars designed for maximum carrying capacity and ease of loading and unloading.

Cane cars carried from a half ton to 30 tons of cane, the load depending on the railway gauge, size of estate and motive power available. American, British and European builders supplied cane cars of their own design throughout the region. Bagnalls supplied a line of cane cars ranging in size from little half-ton capacity four-wheel cars to 12-ton capacity cars fitted with spring axle boxes and steel frames and brakes. Robert

In an attempt to reduce operating costs, and compete with road transport, rail buses or rail cars were used on a number of Caribbean railways. A long way from home, these ex-British Railways Wickham diesel multiple units sit in the station yard in Port of Spain, Trinidad, in 1970. (R.R. Darsley)

Hudson supplied many Caribbean narrow gauge cane railways with cane cars, with the most sophisticated of their larger cars able to be fitted with vacuum brakes, an important feature as cane trains became longer and had to be hauled further. American manufacturers, such as the American Car and Foundry Company, supplied large numbers of cane cars to private and public railways on Cuba and Puerto Rico. For use on permanent, well-laid lines, these cars were very American in style, with bar truck frames, automatic couplers and locomotive-operated brakes. One experienced sugar estate engineer recommended putting locks on the journal boxes of cane cars, as he had found ox cart drivers removing the oil-soaked cotton waste in order to lubricate their cart axles! The largest standard gauge cane cars in general use at big sugar Centrals could carry 40 tons of cane and were 44 feet long and seven feet deep. A train of 20 or so of these cars, not an abnormal load, would require a powerful engine and careful use of the steam regulator on some of the more undulating lines.

Oil, bauxite, phosphate, bananas and timber haulage also contributed to the revenues of Caribbean railways, each commodity requiring its own specialised rolling stock. These specialised cars were either bought in or converted in the railway's workshop and once again this rolling stock evolved by either following the latest overseas practice, or from local experience. While the El Cobre copper mines in Cuba used crude, four-wheeled, wooden ore trucks in the late 1800s, vast amounts of bauxite are now moved in Jamaica by massive steel cars built to modern North American standards.

American-style box cars were usually found on the railways in Cuba, Puerto Rico and in Hispaniola. Purchased by the railway's agents in the United States, the cars featured typical American construction, with American-style bogies and wooden bodies. They carried general freight, bagged or bulk sugar and bulk freight such as fertiliser. Until the almost universal change to oil firing in Cuba in the 1920s, large

numbers of coal cars were imported from America, their main use being the haulage of locomotive fuel from the docks (Cuba has no coal mines) to the various railway yards and depots. English colonial islands often utilised British freight cars that were generally smaller in size than their American counterparts, typically using four wheels, rather than bogies.

In addition to the usual roster of freight cars, some interesting individual ones are listed on railway manifests. The funeral car of the United Railway of Cuba must have been an appropriately stately way for the deceased to make their last journey, and history has kindly drawn a discreet veil over the lunatic car owned by the British Guiana Railway!

The end of the line for the Trinidad Government Railway. In a scene repeated many times in the Caribbean, locomotive No.15, a 1905 Kitson, sits at St Joseph's awaiting the breakers' torch in July 1970. (R.R. Darsley)

Chapter 3

Bermuda and The Bahamas

The Bermuda Railway

The semi-tropical island of Bermuda lies over 1000 miles north of the Caribbean, its nearest neighbour being North Carolina. Only 20 square miles in size, the island is a densely-populated flat coral outcrop, where the main industries are now tourism and banking. The island has been a British possession since 1609, being today the oldest self-governing British Overseas Territory.

The Bermuda Railway Company

Cruise ship tourism, now a mainstay of the Caribbean economy, was responsible for the building of the Bermuda Railway. Furness Withy, an international shipping company, was eager to inaugurate the newly-fashionable cruise ship tourism into Bermuda in the affluent period immediately after the First World War. The company proposed the building of hotels and golf courses to occupy their passengers during their sojourn on the island, and the building of a railway from St George's, where passengers would disembark, to the island's capital, Hamilton. An extension further west would carry passengers into other parts of the island, and promote tourism development.

A railway on Bermuda had been proposed in the late 1800s, but had not been built and transport on the island remained a slow and often tedious process. A Government ban on motor vehicles (except for some official vehicles) meant that horsepower remained supreme and travel around the island, for Bermudans and visitors alike, was firmly rooted in the nineteenth century.

No doubt with the prospect of big tourist dollars as an incentive, in 1922 the Bermuda Parliament accepted, in principle, that a railway would provide visitors with a suitable means of visiting more parts of the island. However, there remained some resistance amongst certain sectors of the population to changing the current transport system on Bermuda, it being felt that boats, bicycles and horse carriages could provide adequate transport, without the disruption to the island's peace and quiet that either motor vehicles or a railway would produce.

However, the idea of a railway persisted and eventually won the day. A 1922 feasibility study showed that a railway on Bermuda could be economically viable, and by 1924, although still with some misgivings, the Bermuda Parliament passed the first Bermuda Railway Act. The Act authorised the construction of a standard gauge railway from St George's, at the east end of the island, to Somerset

Village in the west, providing the railway's investors with a 40-year franchise. Justification for the railway had no doubt been helped by the passing of 'The Motor Car Act' in 1921, a piece of legislation aimed at keeping the smelly and noisy private car, and by extension motor bus, at bay.

The generation of sufficient working capital, problems associated with the purchase of land for the right of way, and the construction of numerous trestles and bridges all took time, more time than had been anticipated by either the railway's financial backers or the Bermuda Government. Construction and financial problems kept delaying the opening of the railway. Finally, after some years of frustration, the Bermuda

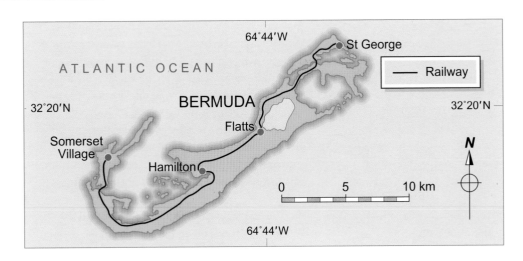

The arrival of a cruise ship in Hamilton, Bermuda was the reason for great activity on the Bermuda Railway. This early 1930s photograph shows the Monarch of Bermuda *tied up alongside Front Street, with one train in the foreground and another in the background on the crest of the hill. (Author's collection)*

23

Railway carried its first passengers from Hamilton to Somerset Village in 1931, on what was eventually to become known as the Western Route. By early November of that same year civil engineering work had been completed on the line joining Hamilton to the town of St George, thus the Bermuda Railway Company was able to offer a regular service the length of the island. The building of the railway and the purchase of locomotives and rolling stock had cost over £1,000,000, a large investment for a 22-mile long railway.

The line was single track working with passing loops located at strategic points and stations along the way. The predominantly coastal route used, while attractive to visitors to the island, would turn out to be a persistent thorn in the side of the company and its maintenance department for as long as the railway operated. While the initial survey had recommended an inland route, acquisition problems associated with the purchase of land for the right of way had forced the railway company to move seawards and build 33 trestles and bridges, some up to 40 ft high, across inlets. Scenic beauty not withstanding, the cost of maintaining these timber and metal structures in a salt-laden atmosphere was horrendous.

In 1932 additional rolling stock and two motorised freight cars were purchased and a programme of track upgrading was instigated, including adding ballast to much of the line. The railway had quickly become a part of the daily life of Bermuda and Bermudans. However, right from the beginning of operations, costs for the railway were substantial and despite a large number of local and tourist passengers, by 1936 the railway company found itself unable to put money to one side for a 'rainy day'. It was evident that the railway would never turn a profit and yet, even while the shaky financial health of the railway occupied much of the directors' time, they remained adamant in their commitment to providing Bermuda with what had become a vital transport link.

Passenger traffic was always the mainstay of the Bermuda Railways. During the time when the railway operated, Bermuda had, as now, few industries, so an extensive freight business would not have been needed. However, it is known that a regular oil tanker service (admittedly usually only one tank car) was operated to serve a local hotel, and during the Second World War large amounts of stores were moved from the docks to the new military bases. As road conditions on the island throughout the life of the railway were generally poor, it is most likely that the railway also offered a parcel and small load service.

The war years, from 1939 to 1945, were a mixed blessing to the Bermuda Railway Company. Large numbers of servicemen, stationed on the island or passing through, used the railway for work and leisure, and large amounts of military freight were carried. Both contributed to accelerated wear and tear at a time when replacement parts, materials and maintenance staff were all in short supply. Even though revenue increased, (in 1947 the railway carried a staggering 1.5 million passengers), it never matched expenses, and by the end of the war the system was badly run down and in need of major renovation. It became evident to the railway's directors that they did not have the financial resources, and perhaps by that time the will, to upgrade the system, and the railway was sold to the Bermuda Government in 1946 for £115,000. It became a public company with the railway's former chief engineer as manager. In addition to providing an attraction for visitors, the railway had become a commuter railway for Bermudans living along its length. It was this public service role that finally propelled a somewhat reluctant Government into its purchase.

Dismayed by the condition of its acquisition, the

Bermuda Government retained an American engineering consultant to carry out a thorough survey of the railway. The consultant's report concluded that it would cost an estimated US$850,000 to rebuild the system to the point where it was safe to reopen for the public, not a lot less than it would cost to convert the existing railway right of way into a public road. The locomotives and rolling stock were in desperate need of repair and many of the railway's bridges and trestles were in very poor condition. The Bermuda Railway was declared unsafe for public use, ceasing operation in 1947. In 1948 the first motor bus fleet arrived on the island and with it Bermuda entered a new, but not necessarily better, era of mass transit.

The railway was dismantled in 1948 and track, locomotives and rolling stock went to British Guiana, there to rise, like the Phoenix from the ashes, and provide a valuable transportation service for the people of that country for many years to come.

When the Bermuda Government retained a Mr Foxlee to carry out a railway feasibility study in 1922, Foxlee proposed the use of a narrow gauge system of 3 ft 6 in and the use of steam tank engines. While there seemed to be few, if any, complaints about the adoption of narrow gauge (it would have made economic and technical sense), great concern was raised over the pollution likely to be caused by the steam engines, so when the Bermuda Railway opened

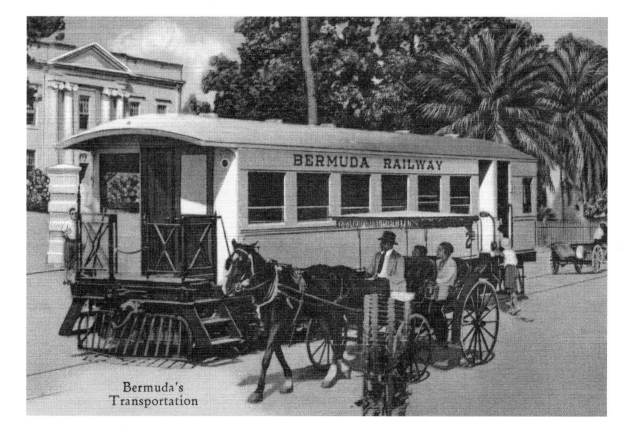

Bermuda's Transportation

Taken from a wonderful hand–tinted postcard, this c.1936 photograph shows one of the Bermuda Railway composite motor coaches in Hamilton. With their primrose yellow bodies, black underframes and white roofs, these cars would have provided a splash of colour as they traversed the island. (Author's collection)

it used internal combustion engine locomotives.

The initial roster of rolling stock on the railway comprised six petrol-engined motor coaches built by English Electric in Preston, England on behalf of the Drewry Car Company. Drewry began supplying petrol-engined rail cars in the early 1900s and always used other manufacturers to build their cars; English Electric began building for the company in 1930. The Bermuda cars were a new direction for Drewry as they were larger than previous models and fitted with a five-speed, pre-selective, epicycle gearbox. Prior to the Bermuda order, Drewry had supplied rail cars to the Barbados Government Railway. The Bermuda cars carried 42 passengers in first and second class accommodation.

Two motor freight locomotives from the same builder were also on the original roster, having similar specifications to the passenger cars except they had two large freight doors and could carry a load of 10 tons. In 1932 two motor loco/freight vans also by English Electric, *City of Hamilton* and *Towne of St George*, were added to the fleet. These gasoline-powered locomotives usually hauled a rake of 'toast rack' or Pullman passenger coaches for both tourist trains and general passenger work.

Two diesel-electric locomotives joined the railway in 1942 and 1943. These 300 hp locomotives were conversions by Cummins of former Brill G-M cars, possibly being provided through the agency of the US Army. A petrol-engined 0-4-0 60 hp 'Planet' locomotive, formerly belonging to contractors Balfour Beatty, was used as a yard shunter with a petrol-engined 'speeder' rounding out the locomotive stable.

Rolling stock consisted of 13 passenger cars, described as 'Pullman', fitted with wicker chairs, and 'toast rack' cars with seat-backs that could be moved from one side to the other so passengers were always facing the direction of travel. In addition to the 5000 gallon oil tank car previously mentioned, the Bermuda Railway had a number of open wagons and flat cars, and these were heavily used during the Second World War for the movement of materials from the dock to the various military installations.

The Ferry Reach Railroad

Even though the Bermuda Railway was not allowed to run steam locomotives, well-known and very wealthy Bermudan resident Vincent Astor was!

Astor had a large estate at Ferry Reach, on the island's west end. In 1934 a 2 ft 0 in gauge railway was built for him, running from his home at Ferry Reach to a point beside the Hamilton-St George line of the Bermuda Railway. Apparently, Mr Astor delighted in firing up the 2-6-0 steam locomotive built for him by the Baltimore & Ohio Railway as a copy of one of their locomotives. The short line was also equipped with a battery-powered, double-ended, locomotive and passenger cars. House guests were often collected from the Bermuda Railway halt by the steam-hauled train driven by Mr Astor, complete with driver's cap!

The Ferry Reach property changed hands several times after Astor's ownership, with the railway falling into disuse, the subsequent owners obviously not sharing Mr Astor's affinity for railways (he was a director of the Baltimore & Ohio Railway). While the remains of the steam locomotive and some of the track are apparently still on the property, the railway effectively finished operating in 1962 when the crash of an American military jet into the garden caused severe damage to buildings and the railway line.

The Bahamas

Located about 50 miles off the coast of Florida, the Bahamas archipelago consists of almost 600 flat coral islands, covering an area of over 5000 square miles. While the islands are generally too dry for any substantial agriculture, a number had considerable forests of Long Leaf or Caribbean pine, and locations where sea salt could be manufactured. Both provided several of the Bahamas islands with a history of railway use that goes back to the 1860s.

Timber has been cut and exported since the early days of settlement in the Bahamas. The Bahamas Timber Company obtained a 100-year licence to cut pine timber on the islands of Abaco, Andros and Grand Bahama, and by 1906 had established a substantial saw mill, logging railway and company town at Wilson City, in the centre of the island of Great Abaco. Most of the lumber produced in the years just prior to the First World War went to Cuba; the sawmill was producing 15-18 million board feet of lumber annually. As timber was cut the railway had to be extended and by 1916, with trees too far away from the saw mill to be hauled economically, the company was in financial trouble. The Wilson City mill was closed, and a new saw mill and camp was built at Norman's Castle, north of the original location, and a new railway was laid. Harvesting ended on Great Abaco in 1943, when all the large timber had been cut.

The Abaco Lumber Co. moved logging operations to Grand Bahama in 1944. A new saw mill and camp were built five miles east of Hawksbill creek in an area later called Pine Ridge. A one and a half mile long 3 ft 0 in gauge railway was laid to connect the new mill with the dock on the north coast. Steam powered the railway, skidding machinery and saw mill, with the machinery most likely being brought from Great

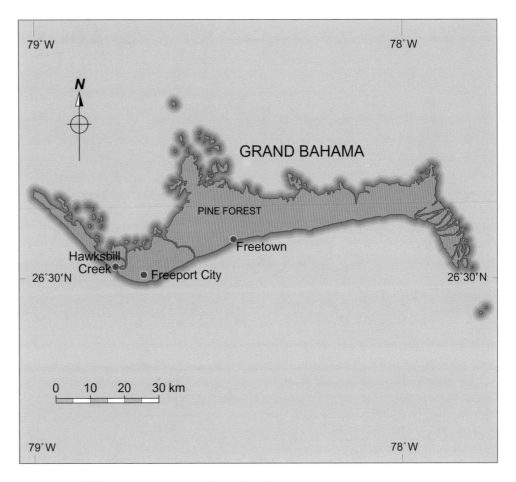

Abaco. In addition to the permanent line to the dock, about 15 miles of light temporary track was laid and re-laid as felling moved further eastwards. The company was purchased by an American investor in 1946, and all steam equipment was replaced by diesel power except the locomotives, which were still running in the early 1950s. The company obtained a concession in the early 1950s to supply the National Coal Board in England with pit props, and a new railway link was built between the saw mill at Pine Ridge and the south shore harbour.

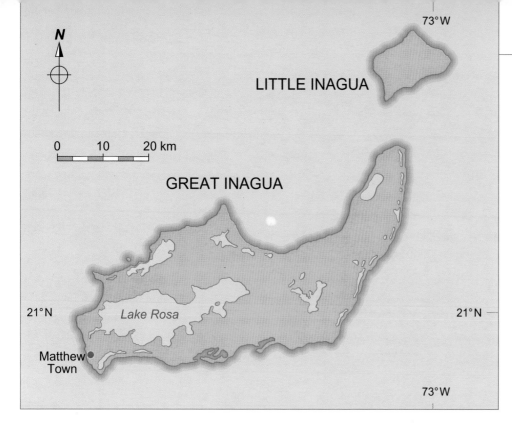

A variety of locomotives, both steam and diesel, were used over the years in the Bahamas' timber industry. The original locomotives of the Bahamas Timber Co. appear to have been two products of the Vulcan Ironworks, an 0-4-4 tank and a 2-6-0 tender locomotive. A Shay geared locomotive was purchased in 1912.

At least four and possibly five Climax geared type A and B locomotives were used by the Bahamas Cuba Co. (probably a successor to the Bahamas Timber Co.). These 3 ft 0 in gauge locomotives would have been ideal for use on the temporary tracks utilised within the pine forests. The boiler of one of the Climax locomotives, thought to be number 5, exploded as a result of the driver screwing down the safety valve in order to build up a head of steam for work after lunch. The official report of the accident surmised that the boiler water level was very low as the result of the excessive steam generation during the lunch break,

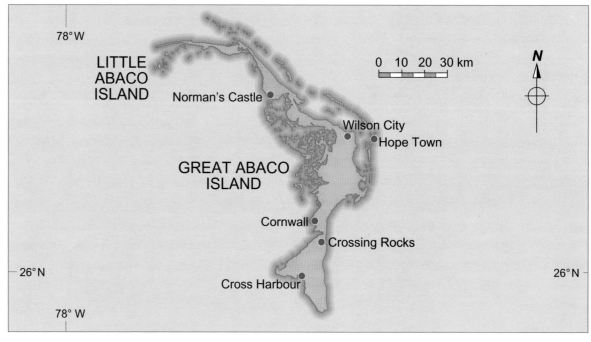

Locomotive No. 3 of the Bahamas Timber Co. was a 28-ton, two-truck Shay geared locomotive supplied in 1912. (Allen County Historical Society, Lima, Ohio)

and when the driver realised and in a panic began to replenish the water the boiler exploded, killing himself and four bystanders.

Harvesting sea salt was a long tradition in the Bahamas, and over the years a number of companies were established to supply salt to North America for the preservation of food before the days of refrigeration. Of all the Bahamian islands, Great Inagua seems to have been the most successful in pursuing this industry, with commercial salt harvesting commencing on the island in the 1840s. In 1865 the short-lived Inagua Tramway and Salt Company was formed, the tramway being mule-powered. The company failed in 1870 and large-scale salt production was not revived until the early 1930s. In 1936 the West India Chemical Co. began production on the south west of the island near Matthew Town. The company was purchased by Morton Salt Co., now Morton International Co., in 1954 and continues to produce salt from about 1200 acres. The tramway had a number of 2 ft 6 in gauge Brookville 4wDM and

4wDH locomotives, the last one delivered in 1962.

Even though rainfall in the islands is sparse and spasmodic, agricultural crops were tried at various times in the Bahamas, and in 1895 the Andros Fibre Company planted 600 acres of former pine scrub land with agave near Mastic Point on Andros, the largest of the Bahamian islands. The fibre produced in the leaves of the agave is used to produce sisal. Contemporary reports of the operation mention a seven-mile-long railway. The project was short lived, however, and Neville Chamberlain, who was managing the project for his father, went on to other things. No account of the railway has been located to date, although it is possible that steam locomotives could have been used as, unlike many other Bahamian islands, Andros has good supplies of fresh water.

One enigmatic railway puzzle in the Bahamas is a barge with remains of a locomotive and several railroad cars that now sits on the sea bottom just off Eleuthera Island.

Chapter 4

Cuba

NTRAL RAILWAY STATION, HAVANA,

Located 90 miles south of the Florida Keys, Cuba is the largest of the Caribbean islands. With a land mass of over 42,000 square miles, almost the size of England, and a current population of almost 11 million, Cuba remains the world's largest producer of cane sugar, contains 10 per cent of the world's known nickel deposits and has a burgeoning tourism industry.

Aligned east to west, Cuba is a long, thin island containing large areas of flat, fertile land, highly suitable for the cultivation of sugar cane and the laying of railways. Today Cuba remains the only island in the Caribbean that operates a scheduled public railway service, an unbroken record since 1837.

From 1492 until the Spanish American War in 1898, Cuba was a Spanish possession. After the war Cuba was governed by an American military administration until 1902, when the independent Republic of Cuba was established. At the time of writing, the anti-Castro American trade embargo with Cuba remains in force, affecting not only the daily lives of Cubans, but also the operation of the island's public service and sugar cane railways.

Train travel remains the most affordable, and often only, travel option for Cubans today, and until economic conditions improve this will probably remain the case. A local appreciation for the potential of tourist railways, no doubt initiated by the popularity of

tour groups visiting the remaining steam-powered cane railways, will probably ensure that railways remain a prominent and important feature of the Cuban landscape for many years to come.

The extent and complexity of Cuban railway history means that only an overall picture can be given of the railway's evolution in Cuba and of present-day operations. However, it is hoped that this brief overview will provide a suitable introduction.

Public railways in Cuba

The realisation that mules, ox carts and poor roads were not conducive to the continued profitability of the Cuban sugar economy became evident after the fall of the price of sugar in the late 1820s, primarily as the result of the introduction of sugar beet in Europe. As the world price of sugar continued to fall the enormous cost of road transport within Cuba, not an economic factor when sugar prices were high, reduced further the planter's profits. This, combined with the increased cost of illegal slaves, precipitated a move by the owners of sugar estates in the Havana area to develop a railway system. While Cuban railways later carried passengers, sugar cane and general freight, the initial incentive for the development of a railway system on the island was to reduce the cost of

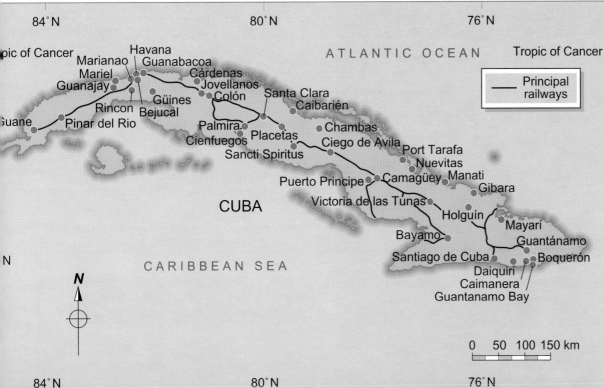

Principal
railways

ATLANTIC OCEAN

Tropic of Cancer

pic of Cancer

Havana
Marianao   Guanabacoa
Mariel
Guanajay   Cárdenas
                Jovellanos
    Rincon   Colón   Santa Clara
    Bejucal   Güines   Caibarién
Guane   Pinar del Rio
                    Palmira   Chambas
                    Cienfuegos Placetas
                                Ciego de Avila
                    Sancti Spiritus   Port Tarafa
                                        Nuevitas
                Puerto Principe   Camagüey Manati
        CUBA   Victoria de las Tunas   Gibara
                                                    Holguín
                            Bayamo   Mayarí
    CARIBBEAN SEA   Guantánamo
                            Santiago de Cuba   Boquerón
    N   Daiquiri
                                Caimanera
                            Guantanamo Bay

0   50 100 150 km

A diesel and steam double-
headed cane train runs through
the cane fields surrounding Central
Reynold Garcia, Mantanzas, Cuba,
May 1998. (Author's collection)

transporting barrels of sugar, rum and molasses to the coast for export.

After a number of false starts (often the result of political conflicts, later to become a notorious feature of railway development in Cuba), Spain authorised the construction of the Havana-Güines railway. A loan was floated in England (foreshadowing later substantial English ownership of Cuban railways), and in 1835 Alfred Cruger, an American engineer, arrived in Cuba to begin surveying for the line. After overcoming considerable difficulties and with much delay, the first section of this railway, to the town of Bejucal, was open for traffic in November 1837. Cuba had become the seventh country in the world to have a railway, eleven years before Spain.

The connection was made from Bejucal to Güines the following year, providing a rail link between local sugar factories and the port of Havana. In 1842 the railway was sold by the Government at public auction. Once in private hands, the railway began an expansion of the line that would see Havana connected with Matanzas, a sizeable port town about 60 miles to the east of Havana, in May of 1863. The railway age had begun in earnest in Cuba.

The success of the Havana-San Julian de Güines railway was not wasted on the merchants and plantation owners of Cuba. At the time most sugar estates were located as close to coastal areas as possible, allowing the products of the factories to be moved to Havana for export by coastal trading vessels, or to the south of the capital, where the distance by road to the port was manageable by cart or pack animal. Isolated settlements such as Matanzas realised that not only would they suffer as ports if they were not connected to the interior by rail, but also that railways that ran through as yet uninhabited areas could help promote development. Competition between towns soon led to a number of public railways being constructed, each with the aim of enhancing or maintaining a competitive edge amongst the landowners and merchants of the area. And it was usually local estate owners, along with overseas banks and Havana merchants, that provided the financing for many of the railways built between 1838 and 1852.

Mining interests in the island also got caught up in this 'railway mania' and by 1844 the Ferrocarril del Cobre was serving the copper mines of the El Cobre area on the south-east coast of the island. This area was later to be the site of extensive mining and railway development, but the little F.C. del Cobre, with its mixture of rope haulage and donkey power, was a very successful precursor of this later important sector of railway development.

Wherever railways were built, the expansion of sugar estates followed, with the transport of sugar, rum and molasses to ports becoming the mainstay of

The new FCC station at Matanzas was built on the edge of town. Here, the west and estbound trains meet in the late afternoon, the eastbound train being hauled by a Canadian-built, Montreal Locomotive Works 2,600 hp diesel locomotive. (Author's collection)

railway business. At this stage in the evolution of the Cuban railway industry, the transport of cane to the factories was not envisaged, as only relatively small amounts of cane were required for the many small, traditional, sugar mills in use at the time. This cane was easily transported the relatively short distances from field to factory by ox cart. Theoretically, by the 1850s, it was possible to travel over large areas of western Cuba by train. However, the passenger service was disjointed and infrequent, with most travellers preferring the traditional stage coach or coastal steamer services.

By the 1850s the 50 or so miles of new railway built each year for the previous two decades began to decline, reflecting a downturn in the sugar economy of the island and the resulting lack of capital necessary to fund construction. However, a decade later the situation had improved somewhat, and railway construction recommenced again in earnest with the result that, by 1863, almost all but the most isolated areas of Cuba were served by railways. In that year over 700 miles of track, predominantly standard gauge, were operated by no less than 21 railway companies, with the island having more miles of track per person than England. Finally, passenger rail travel, at least in the western provinces of the island, had become a viable alternative to road or sea travel.

Considerable improvement had been made to the permanent way, train operations and equipment by the late 1800s, despite some volatility within Cuba. Better quality, heavier rail was introduced, local hardwood sleepers replaced imported softwoods and track was set in a gravel or stone ballast. The gradual introduction of the telegraph in the 1850s improved operating efficiency on the single-track lines by allowing more efficient use of passing loops, while the introduction of larger locomotives and bogie passenger cars, began to have a beneficial effect on timetables and passenger comfort. However, irrespective of these much needed improvements, the haulage of freight continued to generate far more revenue for the railways than did passenger fares. It became evident by this time that the introduction of the railway, and not the concurrent introduction of steam-powered sugar mills, had begun the industrialisation of the island.

By 1868, with 700 miles of railway track, the scene was being set for further expansion. But the latter part of the nineteenth century was not kind to Cuba, the essential sugar economy of the island falling victim to the wars of independence that began in late 1868 and continued off and on with various levels of ferocity until they were ended by American military intervention in the Cuban-Spanish conflict in 1898. The widespread destruction of sugar mills, the burning of cane fields, sabotage on the railways and substantial loss of life had left the country reeling, both economically and socially.

The movement of Spanish troops throughout the island during the armed conflicts of the late nineteenth century had been greatly facilitated by the railways, but it remained evident through these troop movements that Cuba still lacked a unified rail transportation system. It was still not possible to travel directly east-west by rail on one system, and while north-south rails connected sugar mills to coastal ports, the central 'spine' of the island lacked an adequate rail service and the two main cities, Havana and Santiago de Cuba, were not connected by a direct rail link. It was not until 1863 that a plan was formulated that would see the central towns of Santa Clara, Puerto Principe and Bayamo linked into a single system where passengers did not have to change trains. A continuous link between east and west would be forged. However, economic conditions in the country at the time, combined with opposition to the formation of a central railway by the powerful coastal shipping lobby, ensured that the advent of a true universal railway system in Cuba did not happen. It would take a new century and a substantial political and economic change in the country before this dream could become a reality.

Into the twentieth century

With the initial encouragement of the American military administration, and then the Government of the newly-formed Republic of Cuba, priority was given to the resuscitation and development of the island's railway system; a renewal that was aided and abetted in many cases by the influx of American capital, which in turn eventually led to extensive American ownership of Cuban railways. In addition to this re-birth of the Cuban railway system, two other significant and long-reaching events, the establishment of the central railway and the consolidation of small railways, took place in the early years of the twentieth century.

The building of a central railway, one that would connect the east and west of the island through a 'central' corridor, was encouraged by the economic expansion resulting from the American presence on the island in the early 1900s. It was felt that this railway, once established, would open up large areas of the Cuban hinterland to agriculture and settlement.

Politics and self-interest, as expected, made implementation of the plan a slow affair, and it was not until the appearance of William Van Horne in Cuba that real progress began. A legendary railway figure in North America (he had been in charge of the Canadian Pacific Railway project that connected the east and west coasts of Canada), Van Horne soon gave the project focus by establishing a board of directors that included amongst others well known railway man Henry M. Flagler of Florida, and initiated surveys and construction work.

Actual work on the central line began during the time of the American military administration, and continued when the Republic of Cuba was formed in 1902. By early December of that year the railway, calling itself the Ferro-Carril de Cuba, was advertising through passenger services between Santiago de Cuba and Havana via Victoria de Las Tunas, Puerto Principe, Ciego de Avila, Placetas and Santa Clara. The passenger service quickly became an important part of company revenue. A year later the railway was offering a 24-hour Pullman sleeping car service between the two main cities, a journey that had previously taken a week by sea. Prior to the First World War the Cuba Railroad had just over 600 miles of track, 58 locomotives, 65 passenger cars and over 1400 freight cars. In addition, either through the outright purchase of land or the building of branch lines, the company had seen the development of much of the land through which the line ran, providing it with both freight and passenger services. While the railways in the west of the island remained firmly in English hands, Van Horne and his American partners were slowly building up extensive American ownership in the central and eastern parts of the island. The Cuba Railroad was judged to be a success, continuing independent operations until the formation of the Consolidated Railway in the 1920s.

The development of Cuban railways from 1837 to the late 1870s had been fast and furious, but by the latter part of the 1800s it was becoming evident that many of the small, privately-owned lines were financially precarious. Loans, usually from foreign sources, became difficult to repay, with the survival of many of the lines being put in jeopardy. It became apparent that only consolidation into larger operating units could save many of the railways, and this process began in earnest with the formation of the United

Built in the early 1900s the Central Railway Station in downtown Havana, now somewhat less regal, continues to be the terminus for suburban and long-distance rail travel in Cuba. (Author's collection)

Railways of Havana in 1889. Brief descriptions of this merger and others, along with short histories of some of the other main railways in Cuba follows.

In 1889 several small, private lines combined to form the somewhat unwieldy-named 'Bank of Commerce, United Railways of Havana and Regla Warehouses'. The Regla Warehouses had been built in 1843 across the bay from Havana, and at the time were the largest concentration of sugar warehouses in the country. Rail access was critical to their success, and the merger was an attempt to monopolise the sugar traffic into the warehouses. After the withdrawal of the Bank of Commerce in 1898, the company became English-owned and was known as 'The United Railways of Havana & Regla Warehouses (Ltd). Further expansion saw the acquisition of a number of other independent lines, and by 1920, on merging with

the Western Railways of Havana (Ltd) and the Cuban Central Railways (Ltd), the United Railways of Havana operated almost 2000 miles of track.

The railways that combined to form the United Railways of Havana were as follows:

- The Mariano & Havana Railroad Co. (1858). This standard gauge line of 21 miles connected Havana with the town of Marianao where wealthy Havana families were establishing summer houses. A further extension to La Lisa provided a link with the Havana Central. The line was electrically operated by the mid-1920s.

- The Matanzas Railroad (1841) has a special place in Cuban railway history because its first locomotive, a 4-2-2 built by Rogers, Ketchum & Grosvenor of New Jersey in 1843, is preserved at the Central

▶ While perhaps not the most attractive of locomotives, this useful Baldwin electric double ender was supplied to the Havana Electric Railway in 1914. Much of the railway traversed city streets, accounting for the wire and rope 'people catchers' at each end! (Railroad Museum of Penna. (PHMC) H.L.Broadbelt collection)

▶ A Montreal Locomotive Works diesel locomotive stands ready to depart with an afternoon cross-country passenger train, from Havana Central Station, May 1998.

Station in Havana. The locomotive, named *La Junta*, hauled the inaugural train on the Matanzas Railway in November of 1843. Of standard gauge, the line was absorbed into the United Railways system in 1906.

- The United Railway Co. of Cardenas & Jucaro (1857) evolved from the amalgamation of two shorter lines, the Cardenas section of which was in operation in 1839. It was absorbed into the United system in 1906.

- The Havana Central Railroad Co. (1905) was a relative late-comer to the Cuban railway scene, purchasing the right of way of the Insual Railway. By 1923 a total of 63 miles of track and street railway had been constructed, with the company operating

the former Cuban Electric Railway Co. system between Regla and Guanabacoa. By the mid-1920s suburban electric trains were operating a service over parts of the line, from Havana south to Rincon. This was a busy commuter line, carrying over three million passengers in 1921. The railway was absorbed into the United Railways system in 1907.

- The Havana Terminal Railroad Co. began operating in 1912 with the sole purpose of working two and a half miles of track at the extensive terminal facilities of the Central Station in Havana.

- The Western Railways of Havana Ltd (1892) operated as the Western Division of the United Railways on amalgamation, running about 150 miles west from a station in Havana to the towns of Pinar del Rio and Guane. Beginning operation as the Ferrocarril del Oeste the railway acquired its new name when purchased by English owners in 1892. It became a part of the United system in 1912.

- The Cuban Central Railways (1851) began operating between Cienfuegos and Palmira. Subsequent extensions saw the line reach its planned terminus at Santa Clara in 1860. In 1894 the amalgamation of several small lines formed the United Railways of Cariarien and in 1899 this line, the Cienfuegos to Villa Clara Railroad and the Sagua Railway combined to form the Cuban Central Railway (Ltd). This in turn was absorbed into the United Railways of Havana in 1920, adding an additional 363 miles to the system.

- The 2 ft 6 in gauge Caracas Railroad, a privately owned 53-mile system, provided some passenger, but mainly freight and cane haulage services, between a number of sugar Centrals in the surrounding area. It was operated by the Cuban Central.

On absorption by the United Railways of Havana, most lines lost their individual identity. Almost all repair work and operations were carried out by the parent company shops.

Cuba Northern Railroad

Operating along the north-east coast of Cuba, the Cuba Northern Railway had its beginnings in 1916 when the F C de Moron, the Jucaro-Moron Railway and the F C de la Costa Norte came together. Successful railways in Cuba needed access to a port as the transportation of sugar was a staple money earner, so the railway pushed an extension to Port Tarafa in 1919, giving it access to an extensive port facility. By 1922 the acquisition of other lines had provided the railway with almost 200 route miles. The railway opened up an area about the size of Connecticut for sugar cane cultivation.

Large investment in both new track routes and upgrading of acquired lines, new locomotives and repair facilities in the early 1920s gave this line a most modern and efficient appearance. As a part of the railway's upgrading programme Baldwin Locomotive Works supplied and erected a new 15-stall round house and maintenance shop at Moron in 1923, an ambitious undertaking. However, by the mid-1920s the railway was in severe financial difficulties and eventually became part of the Consolidated system.

F C de Gibara a Holguin

This was a 3 ft 0 in gauge line originating at the Chaparra sugar mill (now known as Jesus Menendes) on the north-east coast of Cuba in Las Tunas province. Later connections were made with the standard gauge Cuba Railroad and the 1884 3 ft 0 inch gauge Gibara and Holguin Railway (now abandoned). The line was owned by the Chaparra Sugar Co. Track route was a little over 56 miles.

This delightful 1907 vertical boilered 2-2-2 inspection car (complete with wicker seats for the officials) was one of two built by Baldwin for the Chaparra Sugar Company railway. While the engineer and fireman would have found it hot work, the railroad officials would have enjoyed a cool ride. (Railway Museum of Penna.(PHMC) H.L. Broadbelt collection)

F C de Caibarien a Moron

Located to the north-east of Santa Clara, Villa Clara province, this narrow gauge line connected Caibarién with the town of Chambas to the south-east, via Yaguajay.

F C de Tunas

In Las Tunas province the Manati Sugar Co. owned and operated Manati Central, now known as Angelia Libra, and the 39-mile-long, standard gauge F C de Tunas S.A. which connected the port of Manati with the town of Victoria de las Tunas, where there was a connection with the east-west line of the Cuba Railroad. The railway had one Pullman car and 250 cane cars in the early 1920s, giving some indication of its main use!

Hershey Cuban Railway (Compania de Ferrocarril Cubano de Hershey)

A favourite of railway fans, the 'Hershey Line' owes its existence to the American love of candy and the rapid growth of the Hershey Corporation in Pennsylvania.

In 1916 the Hershey Chocolate Co. purchased an initial 10,000 acres of cane land 30 miles to the east of Havana, with an additional 10,000 acres being leased. In order to provide sufficient cane to feed the enormous new Central factory, an extensive rail system was needed, and the company obtained permission to build a railway from the Cuban Government. The railway was to link the factory with the surrounding cane fields as well as the towns of Matanzas to the east and Havana to the west via the line of the United Railways of Havana. Access to the port at Havana was of vital importance, as bagged sugar would eventually reach the factory in Pennsylvania by rail, having made the 90-mile sea journey between Cuba and Florida by rail ferry. The acquisition of the adjoining Rosario Central in 1920 provided an additional 24,000 acres and doubled the company's sugar production.

Initially operated with a total of 19 steam and electric locomotives, by 1925 the line was in the process of being completely electrified.

Guantanamo & Western Railroad Co.

For many years one of the Guantanamo & Western's claims to fame was that it hauled all the fresh water needed by the US naval base at Guantanamo Bay! Formerly known as the Cuban Eastern Railroad Co., the line began operating in 1903 out of the town of Boquerón, with the main line eventually extending from here through Guantanamo itself and onwards to a connection with the Cuba Railroad. Total route miles was just over 90, including sugar cane loading spurs. The seasonal haulage of sugar cane and the transportation of sugar to the docks provided the line with a substantial part of its annual income. It became part of the Consolidated system in 1948.

Guantanamo Railroad Co.

Begun in 1855, the railway joined the port of Caimanera with the city of Guantánamo, allowing

A Hershey Electric Railway Brill car, built in 1917, leaves Hershey heading for Caraballo on one of its regular inter-urban runs, May 1998. (Author's collection)

sugar Centrals in the area to have access to export shipping. While offering a passenger and general freight service, the line was primarily for the transport of sugar cane and sugar. Connections were made with Soledad and Jamaica in 1883, and by 1929 the railway had extended its track to the north of Santiago de Cuba.

Consolidated Railroads of Cuba

In 1923 Col J.M. Tarafa, President of the Cuba Northern Railways Co., promoted the Tarafa Act, which, when passed by the Cuban Government, allowed the amalgamation or consolidation of the various American-owned railways operating in Cuba at the time. With the rapid expansion of the English-owned United Railways of Havana, perhaps the American-owned lines felt under some threat of being taken over and the Tarafa Act was an attempt to provide the railways with a framework to meet this challenge.

The initial merger under the auspices of this act was the formation of the Consolidated Railways of Cuba in 1924. The Cuba Railroad Co., the financially troubled Cuba Northern Railways Co., the Camaguey & Nuevitas Railway and the Espirituano Railroad were the first railways acquired, and in the early 1950s the Guanatanamo and Western Railroad Co. was added. The strong American influence in the Consolidated was evident by the list of trustees of the line, which included William H. Woodin, President of the American Car & Foundry which supplied large numbers of rail cars to Cuba, and Guy W. Currier, a director of the Pere Marquette Railway Co. in Michigan.

Located through the eastern part of Cuba, the Consolidated Railroads system operated a total of 1318 miles of track and in the 1940s carried $3\frac{1}{4}$ million

passengers a year, or about 40 per cent of all Cuban passenger traffic.

Ferrocarriles de Cuba (FCC)

Prior to the 1956 revolution there were in effect two main public railway systems operating on the island, with control over these private railways being exercised by the Cuban National Transportation Commission.

Railway amalgamation and consolidation provided some breathing space for the privately-owned public carrier railways. However, by the 1920s severe competition for commuter traffic in and around Havana by buses, and the construction of the central highway begun in the 1930s, began to impact on the railways. Apart from a period during the Second World War, when rail traffic was at an historic all time high, the railways of Cuba did not recover from the increasing competition from road traffic. Even further integration of the rail system, a move to diesel locomotives and rail cars, Government control, fare regulation and eventual Government ownership, could not reverse the railways' fortunes. It was not until the later downturn in the Cuban economy with the resulting vast reduction in the availability of road transport, that the railways returned to some of their former prominence in Cuban life.

Complete nationalisation of all the privately-owned public railways took place in 1960 after the Castro revolution. While large private company identities were retained for some years, by the 1970s further rationalisation had taken place, with the Cuban National Railways operating four separate divisions, namely the Western, Camagüey, Guantanamo and Camilo Cienfuegos. A further rationalisation took place and five, rather than four, operating divisions were established. Service is being improved as

Estación del Ferro-Carril — Caibarién — M. B.
Fotografía "Martínez Otero".

In this c.1913 view a classic American 4-4-0 locomotive, No.9 of the standard guage Cuban Railway, stands at Caibarién station on the north-east coast of the island. The locomotive was a product of the Rogers Locomotive Works. The clerestory coach completes a very American picture. (Geoffrey Hill collection)

resources allow, especially along the main trunk routes, by a programme of realignment of the main lines and the siting of replacement stations to the outskirts of towns. While this has removed the pleasure of entering the older parts of these very Spanish-looking towns by rail, always a romantic arrival, the new station locations allow for faster operating times and room for expansion.

Overall control of the system is from Havana. While the railway is operating under substantial motive power and rolling stock limitations caused by the ongoing American embargo, it continues to offer an inexpensive and relatively reliable transport system for millions of Cubans.

Locomotives on the public railways

A sign at the Hershey Railway station in 1998 proudly proclaimed '*Ferrocarril de Cuba - 1837 1997 - siglo y*

medio de experiencia', (Cuba railways - 1837/1997 - a century and a half of experience), a long history covering the evolution of railway locomotives from rudimentary steam locomotive to main line diesel locomotives, electric inner-urban cars and petrol and diesel rail buses.

The locomotives imported from England for use on the Havana-Güines railway were returned as being unsatisfactory, and debate continues on the reasons for their return. While there is evidence that the locomotives may not have performed as well as they should have, a suspicion lingers that Cruger, the American engineer of the line, was instrumental in their return in order to purchase locomotives from America. Irrespective of the circumstances surrounding this change in motive power, American locomotive builders rapidly gained the majority of the business in Cuba. Baldwin supplied its first locomotives to Cuba in 1838, 4-2-0 tender locomotives to replace those made in England. By 1870 Rogers Locomotive and Machine Works had supplied over 100 public railway locomotives to Cuba. The urgent need to develop export markets for locomotives after the American Civil War witnessed other American builders, such as ALCO and Lima Locomotive Works, becoming very aggressive in this market, to the almost total exclusion of all other nations.

From the late 1870s there was an improvement in operating conditions on many of Cuba's western railways, as they were not so severely affected by the continuing cycle of independence wars and the general economic downturn of the island economy. New rail and better track bed conditions meant that larger, American 4-4-0 and 4-6-0 tender locomotives could be used to provide greater haulage power and faster service. Locomotives used on the narrow gauge public lines were often 2-6-0 or 2-8-0 wheel arrangements,

◀ A standard gauge Baldwin Locomotive Works 2-6-0, built in 1907, waits in the yard at Central Reynold Garcia with a loaded train of bogie cane cars, May 1998. (Author's collection)

◀ American style 2-8-0 and 2-8-2 locomtoives had become the workhorses of Cuban railways by the mid-1920s. This powerful 2-8-0 was built by ALCO for the Havana Central in 1920. (ALCO Historic photos)

▼ A standard gauge Baldwin 2-8-0 of 1920 sits simmering in the yard at Central Rene Fraga, May 1998. (Author's collection)

In its smart red and yellow livery, a type TEM-2TK USSR - supplied Brynansk diesel locomotive and train heads through the yard on the outskirts of Matanzas, May 1998. (Author's collection)

better suited to the lighter rails and slower speeds to be found on these systems. A change from locally-grown wood fuel to imported coal became widespread at that time, reflecting the growing scarcity of local wood as forests were cut down to provide additional cane land.

With the intervention of America into Cuba in 1898, significant investment was made in new railway routes, operating infrastructure, and new locomotives and rolling stock. As track was improved and heavier rail was introduced, longer, heavier trains could be used and larger, more powerful locomotives were needed. Re-powering of the railways became a priority, and by the 1920s Cuba had again become a lucrative market for American locomotive builders, particularly traditional suppliers such as Baldwin and ALCO. Powerful standard gauge 2-8-0 and 2-8-2 locomotives became the workhorses for most passenger and freight traffic. These locomotives were in use until the early

1950s, no replacement being possible during the war years, even though traffic on all the railways was at an historic high. As soon as diesel locomotives became available from builders such as ALCO and Baldwin, they replaced the run-down steam locomotives, with many remaining in operation until the lack of spare parts caused by the American trade embargo sidelined them. Considerable numbers of the redundant mainline steam locomotives were transferred to the sugar Centrals, and a diminishing number can be found today at work in the cane fields during the sugar harvest.

During the era when Russia, rather than America, was Cuba's largest trading partner, locomotives from Eastern Block countries, along with some from Canada and Europe, were imported in order to maintain or enhance passenger and freight services on the FCC.

Electric locomotives were introduced relatively early into Cuba, the availability of current from central generating stations, built and owned by foreign companies, providing the impetus for the development of urban electric railways to serve populated areas such as Havana. Electric locomotives currently form the backbone of the Hershey system, and early American electric inter-urban cars continue to provide passenger services on the Havana-Matanzas system.

Diesel rail cars are still used, especially on lightly-travelled country lines. Many of the diesel rail cars now in use were made in the workshops of the Ferrocarriles de Cuba from parts imported from Hungary. Others came from Budd in the US in the early 1950s, from Brill in the US in 1930 and from the USSR in the early 1990s. A set by Fiat, made in Argentina, is used on the day-time 'tourist' special that runs from Havana to Santiago de Cuba. No trace has been reported of the Mack rail buses that were imported into Cuba in the early 1920s, heralding the beginning of the end for steam-hauled urban and cross-country trains on the island.

While steam is no longer seen on the main lines of the FCC (although development work on a rebuilt locomotive was supposedly under way in the mid-1990s), the operating roster of main line North American and European diesel locomotives, electric and diesel rail buses and the many 'home built' self-propelled passenger cars used as local transportation by many of the sugar Centrals provides those interested in railways, as opposed to only steam locomotives, with much to see of interest. An opportunity to travel through Cuba on passenger trains hauled by one of the world's most varied mix of motive power is an experience that should not be missed.

Industrial railways

Industrial railways in Cuba were concentrated around mineral mines and sugar mills. While little information is currently available about mining railways in Cuba, each winter the sugar Central railways remain a magnet for an increasing number of international railway enthusiasts who flock to Cuba to photograph, video and ride on the largest concentration of working steam locomotives in the world. While many of the island's sugar Centrals are now either closed or operate

▲ Central Limones is now Fructuoso Rodrigues and this fine-looking overhead wire powered electric locomotive, built by Baldwin in 1920, is something of a mystery as there is no record of the Central factory operating an electric fleet. (Railroad Museum of Penna. (PHMC) H.L. Broadbelt collection)

◄ Electric railways were not restricted to urban areas in Cuba. This scene was photographed on the railway to Guanajay, to the south-west of Havana. (Author's collection)

▶ Photographed in 1916 in Lima, Ohio, this two-truck Shay was headed for the sunshine of Cuba. Purchased by the Cuban American Sugar Co, it would travel the whole way by rail. The Florida East Coast Car Ferry Company's car ferries allowed American locomotive manufacturers to ship complete locomotives to Cuba; an advantage trans- Atlantic builders could not compete with. (Allan County Historical Society, Lima, Ohio)

▶ At the Spanish-American Ironstone Railway, Baldwin 0–6–0 tender locomotive of 1908, road No. 55, is about to descend the incline to the lower tracks, with the help of a cable, which can be seen between the rails on the right. (Collection R.R.Darsley)

diesel locomotive fleets, enough operating steam locomotives remain on the island to provide a nostalgic experience.

While copper was the earliest mined mineral in Cuba, the island has tremendous reserves of iron, nickel and manganese. The extensive extraction of minerals became a substantial industry in Cuba in the early years of the twentieth century, with both standard and narrow gauge railways being used to move raw material or refined ore to the primary processing plants or ports.

Copper was mined in the Sierra Maestre mountains of eastern Cuba from the early days of Spanish colonialism. The El Cobre copper mine began operation around 1700. In the 1840s a narrow gauge railway was built to replace pack animals, the eight miles of line ending at the pier in Punta Sal. As the railway travelled through mountainous terrain, an incline was needed at one point to overcome a substantial change in grade. The mine was purchased by American interests after the US intervention in Cuba, with repairs and improvements being put in place and the railway being rebuilt.

Iron ore is found in large quantities in a number of areas of Cuba and the Spanish-American Ironstone Company, founded in the early 1880s, shipped its first ore to the United States in 1895. By the early 1900s the company was operating a number of mines in the general area of Santiago de Cuba. A railway was built to transport ore to a port at Daiquiri on the south coast. In 1907 further massive iron ore deposits were located at Mayarí, almost directly north of Santiago de Cuba. (The site of the mine is still marked on the current tourist map as 'La Mina'). It was at this new mine that the Spanish-American Ironstone Company built two substantial standard gauge inclines in order for the loaded ore cars to reach the line that would take them to the coast, where the ore was processed and loaded into ships.

The Cuban Steel Ore Company, the Juragura Iron Company and the Sigura Iron Company also operated iron ore mines in the Santiago de Cuba area, all using railways to move raw material.

As mines in Cuba were mostly operated by American interests, their railways invariably used American-built locomotive, with Baldwin Locomotive Works seeming to be the preferred supplier. A range of locomotive types were used, from diminutive 0-4-0 saddle tanks to powerful standard gauge 2-8-2 tender locomotives. A number of mines made the transition to American diesel locomotives in the 1950s.

The commercial cultivation of sugar cane began in Cuba in 1548. In the Havana area alone 237 sugar mills were operating in 1792. As sugar cane cultivation spread east and west from Havana, towns and cities and ports developed in its wake, with vast areas of the island being opened up for agriculture. In a period of

An American-built locomotive 2-6-0 is set to haul a loaded cane train to the factory. Taken c.1920, the extensive use of steam railways in the cane fields of Cuba would have been a fairly recent event then. (Royal Geographical Society collection, Cambridge University Library)

100 years from 1760 the average production capacity of Cuban sugar mills grew from 46 tons of cane ground per year to 1176 tons in 1860. While steam ploughing and steam-powered cane mills helped increase cane production, the transportation of the growing volume of cut cane to the factory remained constrained by the use of the ubiquitous two-wheel 'Cuban' ox carts. The inefficiency of cart haulage and the cost of buying and feeding the large number of oxen became a matter of concern to mill owners. When the small traditional factories gave way to larger Centrals, initially in the 1880s as a response to changes in the world sugar market, and later as a part of the American economic expansion in the island, it was evident that another system of cane haulage was necessary in order for these factories to operate at maximum efficiency.

Initially field carts carried cane to loading points at the side of the common carrier railways and cane was loaded by hand into cane cars owned by the railway. Trains of cane cars were then hauled as close as possible to the factory by locomotives also owned by the railway. While the railway companies were not

▲ Baldwin Locomotive Works 2-8-0s remain a very common locomotive on Cuban sugar railways. Looking a bit the worse for wear at the end of a long harvest season, No. 1513 of 1920 was photographed in the yard at Central Australia in May 1998. (Author's collection)

▶ MINAZ (Minesterio de la Industria Azucarera) diesel locomotives sit in the yard at a sugar Central in Cuba. Many factories continue to use rail transport, but with diesels rather than steam locomotives, May 1998. (Author's collection)

entirely pleased about this new turn of events, as they had to have a large financial outlay in rolling stock used only seasonally, and often had to build new spur lines or branches, at least it provided some income and was often a lever to get the factories' sugar transportation business. This new cane transport system made logistical and economic sense, and by 1885 125,000 tons of cane were being hauled to the mills by the railway, in railway-owned cane cars, mostly in the Havana-Matanzas area. Only a decade later most Cuban public railways were reporting a substantial seasonal business in cane transport.

Eventually sidings and branch lines were laid by the railway companies. By 1888 the Centrals had their own cane cars and locomotives, to the relief of the railway companies as the purchase and maintenance of both was becoming a severe financial drain. The introduction of the transhipper, a crane that could lift a full cartload of cane into a waiting cane car, speeded up the movement of the cane trains and brought a major economy to the use of railways for cane transportation. Today, the system is further refined as the cane is cut to shorter lengths at the *acopio* or storage areas before being loaded onto cane cars by conveyor.

As an alternative to ox carts for hauling cane from the field to railway loading points, narrow gauge 'portable' railways were laid. Using 10 ft long sections of lightweight steel rail with integral metal sleepers, these easily moved field transport systems, with a gauge of between 30-50 cm (11.8-19.6 in) could support several cane cars, each holding over two tons of cane, in wet or soft ground conditions. The trains were usually hauled by small steam tank engines, although mules or donkeys were used. By 1879 there were 118 portable railway systems in use in Cuba, mostly built by European or English companies. While effective, they were eventually displaced by the extending network of privately-owned branch lines operated by the factory.

The first common carrier railway connection to a sugar Central was in 1893 when the Australia sugar factory was connected by a spur to the Ferrocarril de Matanzas, giving railway access from the factory to the port in the town of Matanzas. The connection proved to be an instant success, with many more mills being connected to the main line, first by the FC de Matanzas and then by other railway companies. By the end of the nineteenth century, the transport of cane by rail had reached such proportions as to impact upon the regular railway service, and it was mutually agreed by the railway companies and estate owners that the estates would be given running rights over railway tracks and that the estates would take over the seasonal haulage of cane using their own locomotives and cane cars. This is the system that continues today with the

Looking clean and well–maintained in this c.1920 photograph, this standard gauge Baldwin 2-6-2 tank locomotive had been supplied to Central Preston (now Guatemala) in 1910. Small steam tank locomotives, often used for yard switching, were often the first to be replaced by small diesel locomotives. (Author's collection)

locomotives and cane cars owned by MINAZ, the Cuban Ministry of Sugar.

The evolution of giant central factories in Cuba was a logical progression as the transport of cane over long distances became possible by rail. The Manati Sugar Company's factory on the north-east coast of Cuba exemplified the new technology of multi-roller cane mills and processing equipment that squeezed the last ounce of sugar from the cane juice. American-funded, it provided ample evidence of why extensive railway systems were a vital part of these massive factories. When built, just prior to the First World War, Central Manati was the largest cane sugar factory in the world, drawing cane from over 280,000 acres of land. Up to 10,000 tons of cane per day could be ground and during the 1922-3 harvest the Central produced almost 87,000 tons of sugar! Needless to say the transportation of the cut cane to the mill and the haulage of the 535,000 bags of sugar to the nearest port required a substantial railway, and Central Manati was provided with one.

By 1924 Central Manati had a fleet of 29 locomotives, 600 cane cars, 25 tank cars, 163 flat cars, 10 box cars, six passenger cars, four cabooses and four auxiliary cars. The system comprised of 144 miles of

▶Vast volumes of steam were produced at sugar factories. Fireless steam locomotives like this example built by Baldwin in 1917 for standard gauge Central Cunagua (now Central Bolivia) could re-charge their steam reservoirs from the factory boilers. Used exclusively in the mill yard, No.3 was reported working recently. (Railroad Museum of Penna (PHMC) H.L. Broadbelt collection).

Public railways in Cuba remained viable after the Second World War and new locomotives were urgently required. The Northern Railway of Cuba ordered this ALCO model FA diesel locomotive in 1951 for main line service. (ALCO Historic Photos)

3 ft 0 in gauge line and 14 miles of standard gauge line that connected the Central with the company's dock. Most notable in the locomotive stable at the Central Manati was a narrow gauge 2-6-6-2 Mallet built by Baldwin in 1917. What a spectacular sight she must have been hauling a long train of loaded cane cars! Now known as Central Argelia Libre, the factory remains in operation. However, there have been no recent reports of steam operation. Would it be too much to hope that the Baldwin Mallet remains, hidden away in the bush somewhere, awaiting discovery?

European locomotive builders fared slightly better selling locomotives to the sugar factories than they did to the common carrier railways, with locomotives coming from Henschel, Borsig and Orenstein & Koppel, the latter being fireless locomotives. As their name implies, these locomotives, usually 0-4-0s, had a large insulated steam storage tank instead of the traditional boiler and firebox. Steam, generated by burning sugar cane waste, was always cheap and plentiful at the factory and so fireless locomotives could be used in the yards close to the factory. As steam was depleted in the storage tank the locomotive

would return to a charging point for a refill. Fuel costs were saved and the initial locomotive cost was less.

The 1920s were a period of substantial growth in the Cuban sugar industry, and this is reflected in the order books of locomotive builders, as larger and more powerful locomotives were purchased to replace older and smaller types. Many of the steam locomotives seen working at the Centrals today date from the 1920s, many having been 'demoted' to sugar cane haulage with the advent of main line diesels and the nationalisation of the railways and sugar industry after 1960. Nearly all of the steam locomotives remaining in operation at the Centrals today burn locally-produced oil.

Today, many of the Centrals, especially those found in the eastern part of the country, now use diesel locomotives exclusively, both for the collection of cane from the country and for the shunting of cane cars within the factory complex. Most of the diesels are from the ex-Soviet block, but a few came second-hand from other countries and occasional steam and diesel double-headers can be spotted.

As a process of retrenchment takes place in the Cuban sugar industry, small Centrals are being closed and their railway system is lost with the closure. As tourism begins to overtake sugar as the largest earner of foreign reserves, it can be expected that this process will continue and the once ubiquitous Central factory and single track railway line meandering through the countryside could well become a thing of the past.

▲ Beside the mill at Central Granma, two standard gauge 0-4-0 switchers, fitted with replacement diesel engines from Russian tractors, move cane cars around the mill yard, May 1998. (Author's collection)

◄ Central Granma has steam locomotives for main line use, but small diesel locomotives are used for moving cane cars around the mill yard, May 1998. (Author's collection)

Chapter 5

Jamaica

Famous for its Blue Mountain coffee and as the home of Bob Marley, Jamaica is a large island with a topography ranging from a substantial mountain range to flat coastal plains, where sugar cane has been grown for over 300 years. Sugar and sugar-related products such as rum are still exported, but today it is the export of bauxite and alumina which contributes significantly to the Jamaican economy and provides some unique Caribbean train watching.

The Jamaica Government Railway

In 1843 the Jamaica Railway Company, a private initiative, was incorporated and promoted by William Smith of Manchester, England and his brother David Smith of Jamaica. A line survey was carried out and £150,000 worth of £5 shares were readily taken up. While three lines were planned, only one was actually constructed, a single standard gauge line from the Angels, just north of Spanish Town to the capital Kingston on the south coast. This short first venture into railway building cost the promoters over £222,000, in those days a substantial amount of money.

The railway was officially opened on 21 December by a ceremonial train carrying the Governor. A second train, no doubt carrying the less worthy, repeated the same journey later in the day at a sedate speed of 28 miles per hour. Sometime later in December a local paper recorded what must have been the Caribbean's first speeding ticket when Isaac Taylor, the driver of the regular Sunday evening train, was fined £2 'for disobeying orders in having put the train at 40 miles per hour instead of 20, as he had been ordered, thereby causing great alarm and endangering the lives of the passengers.' The sight of one of the 1844 2-2-2 tender locomotives rushing through the Jamaican countryside at 40 miles per hour must have been something to behold!

No doubt the substantial cost of this first railway enterprise slowed other expansion, and it was not until 1867 that another line covering the 11 miles from Spanish Town south and west to Old Harbour was constructed, opening for business in July of 1869.

In 1879 the Jamaica Railway Company was purchased by the island's Government and a considerable amount of public money was invested in repairs and upgrading. The railway began to turn a profit, and by 1881 confidence was such that a 24½ mile extension was built from Old Harbour to Porus, and a further 14½ miles was laid north from Angels to Ewarton, an area that in later years became the focus of the bauxite mining industry. The Ewarton extension

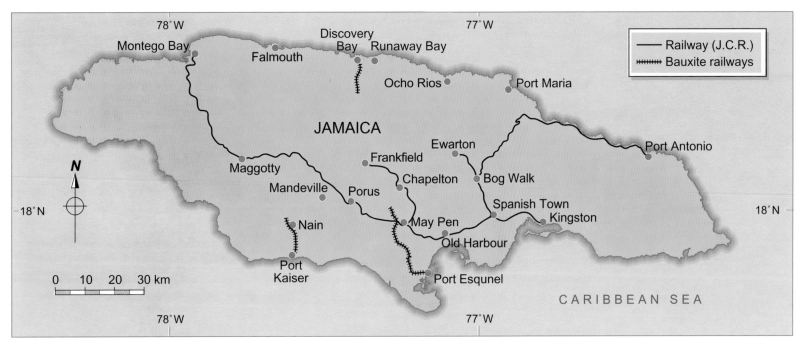

was particularly costly as four tunnels, including the longest in Jamaica at 730 yards, had to be constructed. The successful opening of these extensions prompted a plan to carry out additional extensions of the system to Port Antonio in the north-east and to Montego Bay on the north-west coast.

However, before Government approval was given for this new construction, an American syndicate, called the West India Improvement Company, made an offer to the Jamaican Government for purchase of the railway. In 1889 ownership was transferred to the syndicate for £800,000, an early example of 'privatisation' in the railway business! Incidentally, the new owners were also granted one square mile of Government-owned land for each mile of new line laid. So, with shades of the land acquisition style of American railways, the West India Improvement Company managed to acquire over 74,000 acres of Jamaica.

A Government stipulation at the time of the sale was that the planned extensions to Port Antonio and Montego Bay had to be completed within a set timetable. Given the nature of the terrain (the extensions eventually included 41 tunnels!) either the new owners were not too familiar with the Jamaican interior or they felt that revenues would handsomely repay the railway's purchase price and the cost of the extensions to which they were committed.

Their optimism was not rewarded. The extension to Montego Bay was opened in 1894 and the $54\frac{1}{2}$ mile eastern extension to Port Antonio was opened in 1896. In a process very reminiscent of the early days of the railway, the West India Improvement Company fell on hard times and in default of interest payments in 1900 the railway again became under the ownership of the Jamaica Government. The extensive landholdings that had been granted to the railway company eventually reverted to Government ownership.

By 1911 the Jamaica Government Railway consisted of 194 miles of single line standard gauge main track, with the longest stretch being the 112¾ mile line from Kingston to Montego Bay. The total cost of construction work for the railway to that date had been over £2,500,000. An extension of 13 miles from May Pen to Chapelton, through the lower reaches of the Rio Minho Valley, was completed in 1913 with an extension to Frankfield constructed in the 1920s. Plans to extend the line to Falmouth, an important port on the north coast, never materialised. When the line was built in 1894 many believed that the Montego Bay extension should have gone by this route, that is north to Falmouth and then west to Montego Bay, instead of the winding mountainous route used. Falmouth never did get its railway connection and as a consequence its role as a port declined.

The Jamaica Government Railway served a large and mainly rural population. By the 1920s the 200 miles of main line carried over 636,000 passengers and over 50,000 tons of freight, over 40,000 tons of this being sugar cane, in addition to other agricultural crops such as bananas, oranges and coconuts. Banana shipments became a major part of the traffic into Port Antonio in the late 1880s, beginning the long history of banana cultivation and export from the island and the region. Brought to the Caribbean by the Spanish in 1516, the banana was used only locally until the 1860s when American trading ships began taking them back to the United States. The first bananas left Port Antonio for America in 1869 and a decade later the small town had developed into a major shipping port, almost exclusively exporting bananas. The Boston Fruit Company, later to be absorbed into the United Fruit Company, was based in Port Antonio and banana packing sheds were located all the way along the railway line to the coast. In these sheds stems of bananas were cleaned and packed and loaded onto

special 'banana trains' for transport to Port Antonio. Prior to 1939 the railway's main source of income was derived from the year-round transportation of bananas, with some 270,000 tons of fruit transported annually from the growing areas to the coast for export.

While the banana trade disappeared during the Second World War these years were busy ones for the railway as road transport restrictions meant that the railway again became the only transport alternative, and the establishment of two American military bases on the island provided substantial passenger and freight traffic. In 1952 the Jamaican economy was benefiting from the largest ever sugar crop in the island's history, with the railway generating over £400,000, in revenue from carrying 842,000 passengers and 405,000 tons of freight. As steam-hauled passenger trains were not economically viable, the railway offered rail car services using three, 54-seater, Wickham of England diesel rail cars delivered to the railway in the early 1940s, and a number of smaller, home-built, petrol-engined rail cars. Unlike the later Metro-Cammell units brought from England in the 1960s, these Wickham cars ran well over the indifferent track and required little more than regular maintenance. In common with the Bermuda Railway, however, the end of hostilities brought on a different set of challenges that would see the eventual demise of the railway.

The increasing post-war use of road vehicles, and the development of an extensive, island-wide road system began to spell the end for a rapidly deteriorating railway system, which even the introduction of new diesel hydraulic rail cars and locomotives failed to halt. By 1965 only two 4-8-0 steam locomotives were on the books and all traffic was diesel hauled. Faced with a highly-politicised road transport lobby, a badly deteriorated infrastructure and substantial annual costs, the Jamaica Government Railway closed for good in October 1992. Parts of the line remain in use today, but only for the transfer of bauxite or alumina from the mines located in the centre of the island to the transhipment ports.

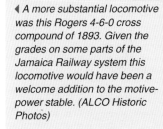

◀ The Rhode Island Locomotive Works, later absorbed into The American Locomotive Company, built this handy little standard gauge 2-6-4 tank locomotive for the Jamaica Railway in 1894. (ALCO Historic Photos)

◀ A more substantial locomotive was this Rogers 4-6-0 cross compound of 1893. Given the grades on some parts of the Jamaica Railway system this locomotive would have been a welcome addition to the motive-power stable. (ALCO Historic Photos)

Rolling stock

The Jamaica Government Railway owned a very mixed stable of locomotives during its lifetime, including conservative and innovative steam locomotives, North American and English diesels and a number of self-propelled rail cars.

During ownership by the Smith brothers the Jamaica Railway Company traffic was handled by 2-2-2 tender, 2-2-2 tank and 2-4-0 tank engines, many built by the famous Scottish builder Sharp Bros. Most of these early locomotives survived into the period of Jamaica Government ownership. However, it was obviously felt that more powerful motive power was needed, and in the period 1880 to 1888 a number of 0-6-0 Kitson of England tank engines were purchased.

Withdrawal of the inaugural locomotive fleet began in the early 1880s, leaving the bulk of the main line work to the new tank engines.

Purchase of the railway by the West India Improvement Company and subsequent route expansion demanded more powerful and faster locomotives. To meet this need a number of Kitson 4-4-0 tender locomotives were purchased from England, and the first of many North American-built engines appeared on the island with the purchase of several Rogers Locomotive Works simple and cross compound 4-6-0s, along with two smaller engines from the Rhode Island Locomotive Works.

▼ *Ready for shipment to the Jamaica Railway, this 950hp ALCO diesel electric locomotive was one of two supplied in 1967. (ALCO Historic Photos)*

Not only did Kitsons supply powerful 4-8-0 tender locomotives in the early 1900s but in 1904 they supplied three handsome and powerful-looking 0-6-6-0 Kitson Meyer articulated locomotives. Given the severe grades, (the maximum being 1 in 30) and curves found on much of the line, a 330 ft radius was quite common, these locomotives would seem to have been ideal. However not much is known of their

operation or eventual demise. A 1925 survey records the number of English locomotives on the line at 17, but does not identify individual types. By 1907 handsome coal-fired Baldwin 4-8-0 and 2-8-2 locomotives were starting to appear on the railway. With tenders carried on two 4-wheel bogies, the locomotives combined power with light axle loading, an ideal combination for the Jamaica railway.

In 1920 the first Canadian-built locomotives appeared in Jamaica. The order for three 4-8-0 locomotives from the Montreal Locomotive Works and a batch of six 4-8-0 locomotives from the Canadian Locomotives Works were the last overseas orders for steam locomotives placed by the railway. Towards the end of the Second World War several US Austerity-type 0-6-0 and 2-8-0 locomotives were added to the railway's motive power. All the railway's steam locomotives were coal-fired and difficulties in obtaining imported coal during the war saw the locomotive fleet burning local hardwood as fuel. The last steam locomotive to operate on the Jamaica railway system, albeit hauling 'specials' in the late 1960s, was No. 54, built by Canada Locomotive Works in 1944.

By the early 1960s diesel locomotive use was prevalent in the system, the brunt of the work being carried out by 750hp English Electric Bo-Bo locomotives. Extensive rail car services, introduced in the early 1940s, were maintained using replacement diesel-powered, sleek and attractive looking Metro-Cammell twin bogie units, of which 22 were supplied to the railway in the early 1960s. Powered by Rolls Royce engines, the rail cars, while very comfortable and capable of hauling a box car as well as carrying a full passenger load, found local conditions very trying. Persistent mechanical problems resulted in the engine and gearboxes being removed and the cars used as coaches, usually hauled by one of the English Electric diesels. There was considerable difference of opinion

between the makers of the cars and railway staff on the reasons for the poor performance of the units. The reality may be that both the design and level of maintenance each contributed to the failure of units that operated adequately on other railways.

Coaching stock on the railway was an eclectic mixture. There were ex-British railway coaches, American-style coaches with open platforms at each end and market cars that were box cars fitted with seats and ventilated by means of windows cut into the body sides.

Sugar and bauxite

While not of the scale of the Jamaica Government Railway, there were other railways in Jamaica. While the cane railways are no more, the bauxite railways of international companies, such as Alcan and Kaiser Aluminium, continue to operate over parts of the original Government railway line.

Large areas of Jamaica are relatively flat with adequate rainfall and fertile soil, ideal conditions for growing sugar cane. Contemporary with other cane producers in the Caribbean, estate consolidation and the building of large Central factories in Jamaica began in the late 1800s. Further consolidation of estates and the construction of even larger Central factories in the early 1900s ushered in the era of narrow gauge cane railways on the island. While never as extensive as those on other sugar producing islands in the Caribbean, the Jamaica estates nevertheless were interesting systems using a variety of locomotives.

The 2 ft 0 in gauge Parnassus *epitomises the basic design for cane railways. Built by Baldwin in 1919, the locomotive, with its short wheelbase, spark-arresting chimney, front and rear wheel sanders and wood-carrying tender, would have been an ideal little locomotive for its job. With everything exposed and accessible, maintenance and repair work would have been easy. (Railroad Museum of Penna. (PHMC) H.L. Broadbelt collection)*

A loaded train of the Kaiser Jamaica Bauxite Co. heads towards the Discovery Bay shipping terminal, hauled by one of the company's Bo-Bo diesel electric General Motors locomotives, May 1998. (Author's collection)

While North American locomotives quickly became established as the main motive power on the Jamaica Government Railway, a cross section of motive power was to be found on Jamaican sugar estate railways. American locomotive builders Vulcan Iron Works, H.K. Porter and Baldwin supplied standard and narrow gauge steam locomotives, as did Andrew Barclay of Kilmarnock, Scotland. Two of the Barclay locomotives, supplied to the order of Jamaica Sugar Estates in 1926, were 2 ft 6 in gauge oil-fired 2-6-0 tender type and were compact and powerful engines for this gauge. In the 1920s Orenstein & Koppel of Germany supplied two narrow gauge locomotives to Monymusk Estate. But the days of steam were numbered and by the early 1930s internal combustion locomotives were being ordered from builders such as Davenport and Brookville in America and Fowler in England supplying 4-wheel and 6-wheel locomotives. No cane is transported by rail today, the result of a contraction in the sugar cane business and competition from road transport.

Bauxite is a naturally-occurring ore containing aluminium oxides. The continuous leaching and drying found in the seasonal wet and dry weather in the Caribbean has produced large bauxite deposits in a number of islands in the region, with Jamaica today being one of the world's largest producers of bauxite and alumina. The transportation of bauxite, alumina, and materials for the processing factories now provides the only rail traffic on approximately 170 miles of remaining railway line in Jamaica. And spectacular traffic it can be!

Four companies, Alcan (Canadian Aluminium Corporation), Alcoa, Kaiser and Reynolds mine and process bauxite in Jamaica. Surface mining takes place in the Ewarton, Mandeville, Maggoty, Nain and May Pen areas with approximately 10 million tons of ore being mined each year, leading to a considerable amount of rail traffic between the mines and either processing factories or docks.

Ore traffic is hauled by large diesel locomotives. Former Canadian National Railway units built in the 1960s by the Montreal Locomotive Works, and General Electric Bo-Bo and Baldwin Co-Co units from the 1950s, many formerly used on the Southern Pacific and Chesapeake and Ohio, operate regular services, providing visitors to the island with ample opportunities to see large-scale Caribbean railway operation at first hand.

Chapter 6

Hispaniola: Haiti and The Dominican Republic

The French-speaking Republic of Haiti occupies the western part of the island of Hispaniola, sharing a common border with its Spanish-speaking neighbour, the Dominican Republic. A populous, mountainous and dry country covering about 10,000 square miles, Haiti manages to survive economically on some sugar and agricultural exports and international aid.

The National Railroad Co. of Haiti

The Compagnie Nationales des Chemins de Fer d'Haiti (The National Railroad Co. of Haiti) had its origins in the railway concession granted in 1904 for the construction of a railway from Gonaïves, on the west coast, to Hinche in the interior of the country via Ennery, St Michel and Massade. In 1906 the company purchased the partly-built Government-owned narrow gauge, Chemin de Fer du Nord, based in the northern coastal town of Cap Haïtien. At the time of acquisition this narrow gauge line had only extended a distance of six miles from its terminal, further progress seemed highly unlikely and the railway was near to closure.

Before long the National Railroad Company was to find itself in financial difficulties, and was certainly unable to complete the connection between Cap Haïtien in the north and Port-au-Prince, the national capital, in the Gulf of Gonâves. In fact, the railway had

only sufficient financial resources to complete about 12 miles of the proposed line.

The proposed introduction of banana plantations along the railway right of way by an American investor saw the amalgamation of the several railway concessions into one, the injection of more capital, and the Government of Haiti becoming a more substantial stockholder in railway development. A new owners' group took over the railway concession, and by May of 1911 a contract had been signed with a New York-based company for the construction of the first 77 miles of 3 ft 6 in gauge track for the eventual Port-au-Prince to Cap Haïtian line. This was to be a 'turn key' operation where the contractor, Caribbean Construction Co., was not only to build the railway, but also supply locomotives and rolling stock. As part of the deal struck between the contractor and financiers of the line, the two cities were to be joined by rail service within a five year period, beginning in 1910.

In 1911 the National Railroad of Haiti became caught up in revolution which swept through the country and while the contractor tried valiantly to continue construction, it was to no avail. By 1913, even though about 110 miles of permanent way was completed and operating, all work on the railway had ceased. By the middle of 1914 it became impossible

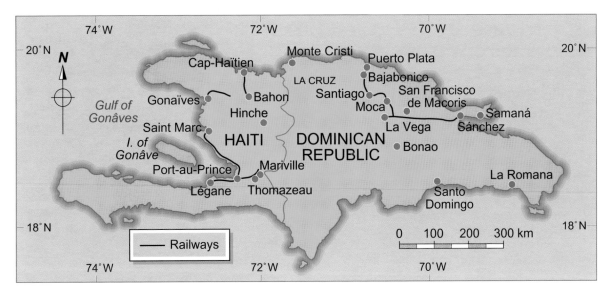

not only to continue construction, but with demolition and sabotage taking place regularly along the line, also to operate.

In July of 1915 American marines landed in Port-au-Prince and began to assist the Government of Haiti in quelling the revolution. In an attempt to help the movement of troops through the country, railway operations were reinstituted, with the repair of the permanent way and lineside structures taking place as and when funds could be generated from revenue. However, by 1920 the railway was insolvent and matters were turned over to a receiver, who found only US$13,500 cash in the bank, hardly a sum to be considered sufficient for the day-to-day operations of a railway!

By 1925 three divisions of the Chemins de Fer d'Haiti were operating, none of them connected. The Port-au-Prince to St Marc division ran for 65 miles northwards along the coast to St Marc. Trains departed from and arrived at Port-au-Prince in what was described as being a large and well-built station made from brick and concrete. The influence of

American railroad suppliers was soon felt on the railway, and on the long Port-au-Prince to St Marc division motive power was provided by three, 4-6-0, Baldwin locomotives. Rolling stock consisted of a number of first-, second- and third-class, clerestory-roofed passenger coaches. It was, however, reported that in all cases on the three operating divisions most passenger revenues came from second- and third-class travel!

The Gonaïves to Ennery division used one 4-6-0 Baldwin and a 2-4-0 Vulcan as motive power. This section was only 20 miles in length, so the motive power and rolling stock requirements were obviously less. Interestingly, a Fairmont 'gasoline motor car' was included in the equipment list for this section. Given the poor revenue generating ability of the Gonaïves-Ennery division it was proposed to abandon the section and use the rail and other materials elsewhere on the system. The northern section of the line that headed south from Cap Haïtien to Bahon was just over 24 miles in length. Two Baldwin locomotives provided motive power and there were three passenger coaches

The Plain of the Cul-de-Sac Railroad was a 2 ft 6 in gauge line established primarily to transport sugar cane and sugar for the sugar factories located around Port-au-Prince, although the line did not enter the city. The line went from the coastal town of Leogane 55 miles eastwards to Thomazeau and Manville near the border with the Dominican Republic. Whilst mainly a freight line, passengers were carried. In 1922 the road boasted a fleet of seven steam locomotives, three motor passenger cars and a mixture of livestock, box, flat and coal cars.

In the late 1940s the railway was operating over 75 miles of line, using seven locomotives, and had 323 cars under lease (most probably cane cars). Parts of this line were, and still may be, operating in conjunction with the Haïtian American Sugar Co. (HASCO) sugar mill.

The railway had a mixture of H. K. Porter steam locomotives, mainly 0-4-0 and 0-4-2 wheel arrangement, and a number of Krauss locomotives that had been used on the Port-au-Prince street railway of the same gauge.

▲ *Five of these solid-looking 3 ft 6 in gauge Baldwin locomotives were used on the Port – au – Prince and Gonaïves branches of the National Railway of Haiti. Locomotive No. 6 was from 1911. (Railroad Museum of Penna (PHMC) H.L. Broadbelt collection)*

and a handful of box cars and flat cars. In the early 1920s receipts from freight traffic far outweighed revenue from passenger traffic, much of the freight carried being agricultural products.

The *Railway Year Book* of 1949-50 records that the National Railroad was operating over 112 miles of track. Information after this date is very sketchy and it is not known for certain when the railway closed; *Janes World Railways* for 1965/66 carries no information on the railway .

Sugar railways

The flat fertile plain to the south, east and west of Port-au-Prince was ideal for the cultivation of sugar cane. Following the development of large Central factories in the area, especially at Leogane, a 20-mile long, 2 ft 6 in gauge railway, known as the 'Haitian American Railroad', was laid through the cane fields owned by HASCO. The gauge was the same as the Plain of Cul-de-Sac Railroad and equipment was interchangeable. In the 1920s the railway had four locomotives and almost 300 cane cars for transporting

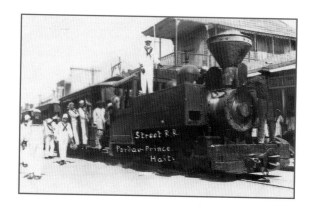

▶ *Sailors from the United States Navy on shore leave in Port -au-Prince pose with one of the 2 ft 6 in gauge 0-4-2 H.K. Porter locomotives supplied to the CF Central d' Haiti in 1909. The original photograph reveals a faded P C S on the side tank, confirming its later move to the CF de la Plaine de Cul-de-Sac. (Author's collection)*

cane to the mills. As noted above, the operation of this railway may have been merged with the Cul-de-Sac system. Other sugar-related railways were located at Fort Liberté on the north-east coast.

The Dominican Republic

Occupying the larger part of the island of Hispaniola, the Spanish-speaking Dominican Republic has a substantial agricultural and mineral-based economy, now combined with a growing tourism sector. While mountainous in places, the northern areas of Vega Real and Cibao Valley contain large tracts of fertile agricultural land suitable for the cultivation of sugar cane. The cultivation of sugar cane for the production of sugar, internal politics, American military intervention and economic investment, and mineral resources have all helped shape the railway history of the Dominican Republic.

Ferrocarril Central Dominicano

Dutch banking interests secured a contract with the Government of the Dominican Republic to construct a railway between the two main centres of the country, Santo Domingo on the south coast and Puerto Plata on the north coast. The railway, to be known as the Ferrocarril Central Dominicano (Central Railway), was to be financed with Belgian money and constructed with the help of Belgian engineers. Work began in 1891, and a 2 ft 6 in gauge line of about 11 miles in length stretched south from Puerto Plata to Bajabonico by 1893, reaching Santiago in 1895. Once the line left the flat plain of Puerto Plata it began to climb steeply, with some parts being 1 in 20, and it was in this section, about two miles out of Puerto Plata,

238 — Les Locomotives étrangères
Locomotive à crémaillère, système Abt, pour le chemin de fer du Central Dominicain

that the Belgian engineers determined that a rack-and-pinion section should be installed. The cost of this section proved too costly a prospect for the Dominican Government, with the result that the Belgian interest in the line was taken over by the Santo Domingo Improvement Co., an American group.

Plans were made to replace the rack section with an adhesion line on a different alignment. However, protracted differences between the Santo Domingo Improvement Co. and the Dominican Government over the value of work completed and cost over-runs resulted in the line becoming wholly owned by the Government by 1908, and the proposed realignment did not take place. A short extension to Moca was completed by the Government in 1908, making a connection with the line operated by the Santiago-Samaná Railroad. Unfortunately, a difference in gauge meant that traffic was not interchangeable, resulting in freight and passengers having to be transferred at the

Gradients at the Puerto Plata end of the FC Central Dominicana were so steep a third 'rack' rail had to be introduced. This is one of the first of four such locomotives used on this section. It was built by Cail of France in 1890-91. They were eventually replaced by geared locomotives from America. (Geoffrey Hill collection)

junction of the two systems. The Central Dominicano was not completed to the original plan and Puerto Plata and Santo Domingo never were connected by rail.

While investment was undertaken by the Government after they had assumed ownership of the line in 1908, considerable damage was done to the line and operating features during the spate of revolutions which took place in the country prior to American occupation in 1916. The rack-and-pinion section of line apparently suffered severe damage by saboteurs during this period. Eventually the high maintenance rack section locomotives were retired and replaced by two Shay geared locomotives. Reputedly the locomotives could each haul about 100 tons up the incline, albeit rather slowly! By 1934 a further attempt was being made to remove this slow and expensive bottle-neck to traffic by the construction of a 12-mile detour with a more manageable gradient. Some indication of the nature of the countryside traversed by the railway is that there were 41 bridges along the length of the line and one tunnel.

Of interest on the line were the French-built tank locomotives for the rack section and an 1899 'Vulcanian' compound built by Baldwin. By the early 1920s the line had a roster of 12 steam locomotives, mostly Baldwin 2-6-0s. The two Shays used on the heavy grades were both 42-ton, two-truck, locomotives with horizontal boilers. All the locomotives were oil fired.

By the 1930s road traffic had badly depleted the railway's passenger traffic and as a result the line concentrated on freight, as the newly-constructed road between Puerto Plata and Santiago, the second largest city in the country, was not yet open for truck traffic. In the 1930s one and sometimes two trains operated between the two towns daily, with freight traffic eventually becoming the backbone of the system. The

economic depressions of the post-Second World War period were not kind to the railway and by 1951 it was closed.

Ferrocarril de Samaná y Santiago

The first railway in the Dominican Republic, the Ferrocarril de Samaná Santiago (Samaná and Santiago Railway), had its beginnings in 1878 when Alexander Baird, a Scot, was granted a concession to build a railway to connect the town of Samaná, on the north shore of the Bay of Samaná, with Santiago to the east. Construction began at Samaná in 1881, but difficulties in the acquisition of land led to the abandonment of this section and a move to begin construction further inland at Sánchez. By 1886, construction of the 62-mile long, 3 ft 6 in gauge line between Sánchez and La Vega was completed, with the section through the Gran Estero swamp being particularly difficult and expensive due to the amount of stone fill required to support the rails. In one section the track was laid on a concrete foundation poured on the bed of the river. While traffic sometimes had to be curtailed over this section during heavy rains, when up to 15 ft of water covered the tracks, it was preferable to the frequent replacement of the washed-out bridge originally used at this site.

Two branches were constructed after completion of the main line. A seven-mile branch from La Gina to San Francisco de Macoris was opened in 1894 and a 34-mile long branch from Las Cabullas to Salcedo and Moca (also the terminus of the Central Dominican Railway) was completed in 1905 and 1917 respectively, work on the Moca branch being delayed by the activities of various revolutionaries!

Although the Samaná-Santiago Railway travelled through flatter country than the Government railway, extensive engineering works were necessary, with over

170 bridges and 200 concrete culverts being constructed on the 97 miles of main line.

Scottish, not American, built locomotives were used on the Samaná-Santiago Railway, most likely reflecting the Scottish ownership of the operating company (its head office was in Glasgow, even in the 1930s) and possibly from the influence of one of its directors, the well-known William Whitelaw of the London and North Eastern Railway in England. Early locomotives were purchased from Neilson of Glasgow, but by 1914 these engines were replaced by three handsome and powerful 2-6-2 tank engines from Glasgow builders, the North British Locomotive Co. Ltd., and these engines provided the motive power for the railway throughout the 1930s. With their outside valve gear, 'cow catchers' at each end and large smokebox-mounted headlights, the locomotives were an attractive mix of British and American styles. Two small Andrew Barclay & Sons 0-4-2 tank engines were used for work on the dock at Sánchez and in the railway yards, and four steam-powered rail cranes were used there for loading and unloading ships and lighters. At one time there had been a roster of about 15 locomotives on the railway, but by the mid-1930s those not cut up for scrap were lying in the yard at Sánchez. In the spirit of progress, and no doubt in an attempt to lower running costs, by the 1930s a petrol rail car was operating passenger services along the line.

By the 1930s two trips were being made, east and west, during the week, with a mixed train consisting of American-style bogie passenger and goods cars. The growing of cocoa developed into a substantial industry along the route of the railway and in the 1930s 30,000 tons of beans were carried annually by rail.

Freight operations gradually became the mainstay of the line, but the development of a highway system in the 1920s and 1930s began to undercut the railway. The fact that the infamous Dominican Republic dictator Rafael Trujillo had significant road transport interests and was not well disposed to the railways did not help the situation! The Samaná and Santiago managed to hang on until 1970, an interesting little railway which never did reach either Samaná or Santiago!

Ingenio Angelina, in the south-west of the Dominican Republic, operated this 1908 2 ft 6 in gauge Baldwin Milan. The locomotive was a compound; note the difference in size between the high and low pressure cylinders. The locomotive survived until about 1960. (Railroad Museum of Penna. (PHMC) H.L. Broadbelt collection)

2753

Little Fiume operated on the 1ft 10½in system at the Caei sugar factory. Built by Baldwin in 1925, this diminutive locomotive was equipped with a large tender to carry its wood fuel, electric headlights (for night working) and a running-board mounted steam pump for boiler feed. The inside valve gear fitted would have been a bit of a mechanic's nightmare in this small gauge. (Railroad Museum of Penna. (PHMC) H.L. Broadbelt collection)

Sugar cane railways

Large sugar Centrals, or *'ingenios'*, began to be constructed in the Dominican Republic in the late 1870s, with the island quickly becoming the second largest sugar producer in the Caribbean after Cuba.

Narrow gauge railways soon criss-crossed the thousands of acres of cane fields around Santo Domingo in the south and Puerto Plata in the north. At least 21 of the new factories were using railways for the delivery of sugar cane in the 1920s. While 2 ft 6 in seemed to have been the most common gauge, other railways ranged from 1 ft 10½ inch at the Italira through to standard gauge, the latter at Central Romana. A number of the lines were of considerable length, the Ingenio Santa Fé, for example, having over 200 miles of 2 ft 6 in gauge main and branch line. Other mills had railways running from 60 to 20 miles in length, with 30 miles seeming to be the average. As with other large mills, both the main and branch lines would be permanent, with cane being delivered to

fixed loading points by carts usually pulled by oxen. American locomotives were generally used on the factory railways, a reflection on American influence and ownership in the country during the American occupation from 1916 to 1924, and locomotive rosters in the 1920s showed a preponderance of products from the Baldwin Locomotive Works and a few Porters. Wood, imported coal and imported oil were all used as fuel for the locomotives.

Even with factory closures and the abandonment of the railways in favour of road transport, over 900 miles of cane railway remained in operation in the late 1980s. Isolated steam operation lasted at least until the late 1960s or early 1970s.

Sugar mills that remain in operation are either privately owned or owned by the Dominican Government. Approximately a dozen mills were in operation in 1997, mainly using a mixture of diesel hydraulic and diesel electric locomotives built either by Plymouth or General Electric.

Banana lines

The Dominican Republic was one of several Caribbean islands that had a substantial banana export business, and railways played an important part in this industry by moving large volumes of fruit from the packing sheds or farms to the ports. Extensive banana plantations were developed in the Dominican Republic around the La Cruz area on the north coast near the border with Haiti, and at Sosua. The latter were abandoned by 1916 but the Manzanillo railway, operated using a Plymouth locomotive, continued until 1966 when the line was nationalised. Finally it was abandoned in the early 1970s when the banana industry contracted.

Falconbridge Dominicana CporA

The Canadian mining company Falconbridge has operated a large open-cast nickel mine and refinery near the town of Bonao, about 50 miles north of Santo Domingo, since 1972. While the mining operation uses trucks to move the ore from the mine site to a storage area at the processing plant, two short railways operate inside the plant.

Calcinated ore is transferred by electric locomotive-hauled hopper cars a short distance from the shaft furnace to one of two electric furnaces, with slag and refined metal, in 40 metric ton ladles, being moved from the electric furnaces to the refining stations by rail. Standard gauge, 80-ton, GE Bo-Bo diesel electric locomotives are used.

An 80-ton GE diesel electric locomotive stands at the head of a slag car train at the Falconbridge Works near Bonao in the summer of 1998. (Author's collection)

Chapter 7

Puerto Rico

The Commonwealth of Puerto Rico, known to many Caribbean visitors today as a cruise ship terminal or air travel hub, is an island of over 3000 square miles with a mountainous interior and flat coastal plains. Under Spanish rule until 1898, when it was ceded to the United States at the end of the Spanish-American War, the present Commonwealth of Puerto Rico remains closely linked politically and economically to the United States.

The Compania de la Ferrocarriles de Porto Rico

The Minister of Colonies of Spain tried to auction a concession for a railway in Puerto Rico in 1880, with the home government prepared to provide financial guarantees as an inducement to bidders. However, the offer was not taken up and the idea of a public railway on the island lay dormant until 1888, when a franchise to build a railway to encircle the island on a coastal route was secured by one Don Ibo Bosch. The railway, to be known as the Compania de la Ferrocarriles de Porto Rico, was to be completed within eight years and again financial guarantees were to be provided by the Spanish Government.

Track laying for the railway began in earnest at three separate locations along the proposed route. By 1892, four years after the agreement was signed, 16 miles of metre-gauge single track connected San Juan, the island's capital on the north coast, with Carolina to the east and with Camuy 48 miles to the west. From Aguadilla on the west coast a line was constructed for 22 miles south to the town of Mayagüez and a further 24-mile section had been completed to connect Ponce and Yáuco on the south coast. In total this 100 miles of track was less than half of the contracted 283 miles. Service on these isolated sections began in 1891.

The American Railroad Co. of P.R.

Spain ceded Puerto Rico to the United States of America in 1898. As in Cuba and the Dominican Republic, this change in political status saw considerable American investment in Puerto Rico. In 1902 operation of the island's railway was taken over by a New York corporation, the American Railroad Company of Puerto Rico. The lease entered into by the Company was to run until January 1957.

In 1899 an observer in Puerto Rico reported that the island railroad would disgrace any American

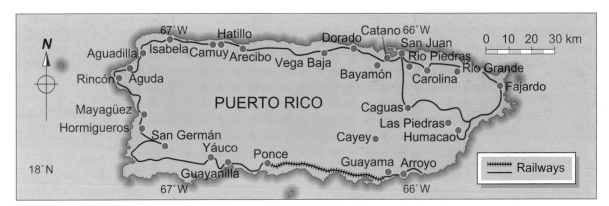

logging or mining region 'so mean and primitive are the cars, and so poorly kept are the engines'. Service on the three completed (but not connected) sections apparently consisted of one train per day operating at a speed of 10 miles per hour. Mail was carried on the train as far as the rails went, and then by either coach or horseback to the next section for transfer to the railway again! Contemporary photographs show small tank or tender locomotives and wooden-bodied American-style bogie coaches being used on largely un-ballasted track.

At considerable cost a tunnel had been built to allow the connection of the Camuy and Aguadilla sections by the First World War, finally linking San Juan and Ponce. Ponce remained the southern terminal for the railway, and while the American Railroad Co. obtained running rights eastwards over the tracks of the Ponce and Guayama railway, it was as unsuccessful as its predecessor in finishing the complete island coastal route.

Investment in new locomotives by the American Railroad included three 0-6-6-0 Baldwin Mallets in 1904, amongst the first built by the company. By 1925 the railroad boasted a fleet of 52 oil-burning steam locomotives, mainly 4-6-0s and small 0-6-0 tank engines, all of American manufacture, over 40 metal-

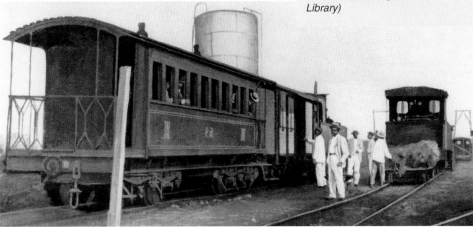

◄ *A busy scene, c.1900, at the Catano railroad station of the Compania de la Ferrocarriles de Porto Rico. This section of the railway ran from Catano, across the bay from San Juan, 48 miles westwards to the town of Camuy. (St Croix Landmarks Society Research Library)*

▼ *The daily train on the San Juan – Carolina section of the Ferrocarriles de Porto Rico consists of a tank locomotive, box car and a third-class coach. Photograph c.1900. (St Croix Landmarks Society Research Library)*

during the train's slow progress through the hot and
dusty cane fields that formed the majority of the lineside scenery. Extensive locomotive and rolling stock
repair facilities for the railway were located in San Juan
and Ponce. Major locomotive overhauls could be
carried out at the San Juan shops.

▲ *The first articulated, compound
Mallet locomotives built by Baldwin
were supplied to the American
Railroad of Puerto Rico in 1904.
Tractive effort 20,000lb, weight
53 tons. (Railroad Museum of
Penna. (PHMC) H.L. Broadbelt
collection)*

▲ *By 1923 the American Railroad
of Puerto Rico had a stable of 52
locomotives. This ALCO was one
of a number of oil-fired metre
gauge 2-8-0s the company had
supplied to the railway. (ALCO
Historic Photos)*

bodied passenger cars and over 1000 freight and cane
cars, the seasonal carrying of cane to the large new
Central factories by now providing substantial revenue
for the railway.

Amazingly, many of these locomotives were still
working in 1947, along with some small diesels. Two
46-passenger steam rail cars were provided by Baldwin
in 1923, the integral locomotive power units having an
0-4-2 wheel arrangement. These steam 'motor cars',
developed by several locomotive manufacturers to
meet the growing competition from petrol-engined rail
cars, were never truly successful and little is known of
their working history in Puerto Rico.

All the railway's locomotives and cars, except those
used for cane, were provided with Westinghouse air
brakes. The interior of the American-style passenger
cars were fitted with overhead fans and louvres above
the windows, both essential for passenger comfort

The dream of a railway around the island persisted.
While it was probably too little too late, a 1921
Government bond issue to the amount of US$3
million was launched to raise the money for extending
the existing railway east and then north from Ponce to
San Juan, via Humacao, Fajardo and Carolina. The
concentration of privately-owned railways in the far
east of the island, such as the Compania de los
Ferrocarrils Puerto Rico, the Fajardo Development
Co. and the Caguas Tramway were to be connected to
form a 'belt-line' railway that would serve the
developing areas to the east and south of San Juan.
However, in spite of Government efforts to promote
the plan, nothing materialised, and the eastern part of
the island remained somewhat isolated for a long time.

The leisurely passenger service offered by the
railway (including an overnight train between San Juan
and Ponce), provided no competition for motor
vehicles, once a decent road system began to develop
on the island in the early 1920s. The emergence of
publicos, private cars used as taxis, in the 1930s offered
a new challenge to the railroad as their drivers were not
above poaching railroad passengers right from the
station platforms! Trucks began to move general
freight around the island as the road system improved,
eating further into the railroad's revenue. It was
evident that business was not going to improve. In
1947 a bankruptcy petition was filed by the company.
Unusually for a Caribbean railway, all the creditors
were paid as the company held large amounts of land,
especially in San Juan, most of which was sold off to
pay debts.

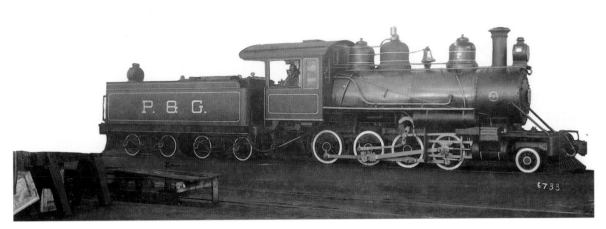

After the sale, the railway was reorganised as the Puerto Rico Railroad and Transportation Company and rail passenger services were discontinued in favour of the transportation of sugar cane. Inevitably, this seasonal business provided insufficient revenue to pay the bills, even though over 1.2 million tons of sugar was produced on the island in the 1950-1 harvest. The company, and the railway, ceased operation in 1957.

Other public railways

As in Cuba, Puerto Rico had several small railways providing passenger services, often in conjunction with the haulage of cane to the 30 factories that began to appear on the island in the early 1900s.

The Ponce & Guayama Railroad Co. was the American-owned successor to the company that owned the Central Aguirre. By the mid-1920s the railway had about 30 miles of metre-gauge single line that headed east through the flat, fertile, cane lands from Ponce to Guayama and whereas some passenger revenue was generated, 95 per cent of the traffic was sugar cane. In the mid-1920s the line owned a number of 0-6-0 and 2-8-0 oil-fired steam locomotives. Access into Ponce proper was via a short length of track

owned by the American Railway, giving the P&G access to the port at Ponce and an easily accessible export point for the numerous Centrals in the area.

The Canadian-owned Porto Rico Railroad Co. (Ltd) was incorporated in 1906 for the purposes of acquiring two railway companies operating in the San Juan area, namely the Porto Rico Power & Light Co., which operated a commuter-type railway in and around San Juan, and the Caguas Tramway Co. The former had a generating station in San Juan and the latter operated an 18-mile-long, metre-gauge railway between Caguas and Rio Piedras to the north. The line between San Juan and Rio Piedras was steam operated, but by 1899 the US administration had granted the company permission to make the change to electric propulsion and widen the track gauge. By 1901 this system was in place and operational, and by incorporating the Caguas tramway system, also converted to electric cars in the early 1900s, provided a direct service operating between Caguas and San Juan, via Rio Piedras, a distance of about 12 miles, using electricity supplied by the Porto Rico Light & Power Company.

The Linea Ferrca Del Oeste was a short line that initially ran from Catano, across the bay from San Juan (what is now known as 'Old San Juan') south and west to the town of Bayamon. Established in 1881, the metre-gauge line also ran a ferry that connected its terminal at Catano with San Juan. The San Juan and Carolina line connected these two towns and the Ponce Light Co. operated a short electric line connecting Ponce with Ponce Playa on the coast. Some reports have this as a standard gauge railway, but as the same company operated a metre-gauge street railway in Ponce, the short run to the port may well have been the same gauge.

The Humaco Railroad operated in eastern Puerto Rico running from Humaco to Las Piedras with a branch to Humaco Playa, a total distance of about 22 miles. The metre-gauge line was unusual in that it used Porter locomotives, a change from the ubiquitous Baldwins found on the island. As its equipment roster consisted of over 300 cane cars of various capacities and one passenger car, it can be assumed that passenger traffic was not a priority for the railway, and it was only the Humaco to Humaco Playa section that worked as a public carrier.

Sugar and industrial railways

With the American takeover of Puerto Rico, investment in the island's cane sugar industry showed a significant increase. Large factories, some capable of grinding 1000 tons of cane a day, were built around the fertile coastal plain. Each factory had its own railway and nearly all of these private lines were built to metre gauge, allowing interchange with the American Railroad of Porto Rico for the delivery of cane to the mill and the delivery of finished products to the island's ports. A number of these private railways had one or two passenger cars, but their use was restricted to the conveyance of employees or a casual passenger service, rather than providing scheduled services.

The Fajardo Sugar Co. of Puerto Rico built a large sugar factory near the town of Rio Grande and to transport sufficient cane for the mill's demand, a railway was to be constructed to the east by the town of Naguabo. As this proposed line was to run in the general area of the Government's proposed east coast connecting loop, the company was required to run a passenger train from end to end of the line, as well as hauling sugar cane and general freight. The 50-mile line was completed by 1910, but the passenger service never amounted to much, and it never did form part of the proposed circular route.

Several of the other Central railways operating in Puerto Rico are of interest. Track length at the mills varied between a maximum of about 85 miles at the Central Canovanas to a minimum of 1.2 miles at the Central San Francisco. Most of this single track was metre gauge, using light rail, laid directly onto the ground. Several Centrals, including those of the Fajardo Sugar Co. in the eastern part of the island, had portable railways using 12-16 lb rail, the Fajardo system having a very extensive system of about 100 miles. Early photographs show dual-gauge tracks entering some mill buildings, the inner track no doubt being the 30 in portable line coming out of the fields.

Baldwin, Lima, ALCO, Vulcan, Bell and Davenport supplied locomotives to Porto Rico customers. Central Cambalache, located at Arecibo on the north coast west of San Juan, operated a fleet of six, two-truck, light-weight Shays and others were purchased by the Cayey Sugar Co. (an 18-ton, two-truck engine) and by Fox Bros. & Co. Given the operating condition and lightness of rail used on many cane lines, the use of these slow-speed, geared locomotives made sense, and it is somewhat surprising that more locomotives of this type were not sold for use in the Caribbean.

Into the future

In the mid-1920s there were almost 350 miles of public service railway and over 600 miles of private railway in Puerto Rico. Evidence of this extensive railway heritage is now mostly gone, and apart from the short, diesel hauled, '*Tren del Sur*' tourist railway that operates along the old cane railway tracks at Arroyo on the south coast, working railways appeared to be a thing of the past on the island.

However, in a surprising and innovative move, construction of an urban light railway was launched in San Juan in July of 1999. To be built at a cost of US$1.65 billion, the railway, to be completed in the year 2002, will hopefully alleviate the dreadful road traffic problems experienced by commuters from the suburbs of a rapidly expanding and sprawling San Juan.

Tren del Sur *operates a tourist train in the south of Puerto Rico with Plymouth 0-6-0 diesel locomotives formerly used on sugar cane lines in the area, August 1999. (Author's collection)*

Chapter 8

Leeward Islands:
St Croix, St Kitts, Antigua and Gaudeloupe

St Croix

St Croix is the largest of the three main islands making up the US Virgin Islands. Originally French, then owned by Denmark until its sale to the United States in 1917, St Croix evolved as a cane sugar producer through animal and wind-powered mills to steam mills. Estates were quite small, and the technology of steam-powered mills was not generally accepted on the island until the early 1850s.

The largest and longest lived of the St Croix sugar factories was at Estate Bethlehem, located to the west of Christiansted. The new factory, known as the West India Sugar Factory, and owned by the Danish West Indian Sugar Company, eventually expanded its production to 20 estates, and cane was brought to the mill by railway. By early May of 1909 a 1000 mm gauge railway, with steam locomotives *Olga* and *Johan*, was reported operating out of the Behlehem factory by the St Croix *Avis* newspaper. The railway and its locomotives were quite a novelty on St Croix apparently, and residents were in the habit of going out to the line to see the action.

The railway's two original locomotives were purchased by Mr Lachmann, managing director of the Danish West Indian Sugar Company, who lived in Copenhagen, and the locomotives were probably named after his children. The locomotives were likely numbered 1 and 2, as by 1913 they had been joined by number 3, a 90 hp 0-8-0 tank engine built by Orenstein & Koppel of Germany. This locomotive is known to have had leading and trailing axles built on the 'Klien-Linder' system to provide more flexibility for a long rigid wheelbase locomotive on a narrow-gauge track with tight curves. Similar locomotives are known to have been used on sugar plantations in Java.

There seems to be no clear indication of the makers of number 1 and 2 and the three known photographs of the Estate Bethlehem steam locomotives show two distinctly different types of locomotives, with the two original locomotives definitely more 'American' looking, with large head lights and bells. Reference has been made to an unidentified 0-4-0 tank engine owned by the West Indian Sugar factory, but no builder has been forthcoming. Whether this locomotive is one of the two originals is not clear. One of the three known locomotive photographs, possibly from a postcard, was taken before 1917 as it is marked D.W.I (Danish West Indies). While not very clear, it shows two locomotives side-by-side outside the Bethlehem factory, and on one of the locomotives what appears to be the name '*Olga*' is partially visible on the tank side close to the cab. Both locomotives have two boiler-mounted domes,

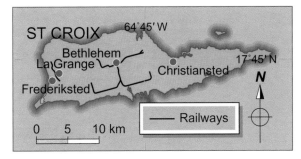

spark-arresters on the chimney and open cabs with a metal roof. On the nearest locomotive the outside cylinders are inclined and the wheel arrangement seems to be that of an 0-4-2.

What is known for certain is that the three locomotives operated on different sections of what eventually became a railway of about a dozen miles length. A north-south main line connected the factory with two lines running at right angles, forming a letter 'H' configuration.. The northern main line split to run east-west just north of the factory, with one line heading east past Fredensborg and Fredensfeld, with the other heading west towards Estate River. The southern line crossed Centerline Road west of Kings Hill (complete with a 'look out for locomotives' sign and crossing gates) and continued south until it reached Estate Infield, where a bridge spanned a small river. Just past the bridge the line split into two, with one section heading east past Estate Anguilla and onwards towards Estates Jerusalem, Hope and Blessing. The west line went past Estates Manning Bay, Envy and Diamond, terminating a short distance from Centerline Road in the area of Estate Mount Pleasant. As no turning 'Wye' is evident on the survey map, the trains must have been 'push-pull' except on the Fredensborg section, where a short spur line is indicated.

The bridge at Estate Infield was either of light construction or very narrow, as apparently the Orstein

& Koppel locomotive, called 'Blaere', could not cross it. The two smaller locomotives brought loaded cane from each of the lower lines to a point north of the bridge, where longer trains were marshalled and hauled to the factory. Contemporary photographs show cane being stacked sideways on the cane cars, making a wide load, so it was most likely the weight of the O&K locomotive was the problem. Refined sugar was transported the few miles to the dock at Christiansted by ox cart or, later, by road, the railway never being extended to carry this out.

Closed during the duration of the Second World War, Bethlehem factory reopened in the post-war period and was the last to operate on St Croix, closing in 1966. The factory was disassembled and shipped, lock, stock and barrel, to Venezuela where it apparently still operates today.

La Grange Estate, located a few miles to the east of Frederiksted, was also owned by Danish interests in the early 1900s and could produce about 30 tons of sugar per day. It had a narrow gauge mule tramway to Estate Williams and south to Estate Wheel of Fortune.

Locomotive No.3 Blaere of the St Croix cane railway was an Orenstein & Koppel 0-8-0 fitted with 'Klien-Linder' axles on the leading and trailing drivers. The 90 hp locomotive was built in 1913. (St Croix Landmarks Society Research Library)

A loaded cane train, hauled by one of the two original St Croix locomotives, on its way to the factory in this scene taken from a postcard dated 1912. (St Croix Landmarks Society Research Library)

In all there were about two miles of track. A photograph of the La Grange factory, taken in the early 1900s, shows a rake of small 4-wheel cane cars standing on a siding; a photograph with a mule and train has not been located. The factory at La Grange continued to operate through the 1930s, when Bethlehem was closed, and utilised cane from Bethlehem's acreage. No connection was ever made between the two rail systems.

A 1937 Brookville 4-wheel diesel-mechanical locomotive was imported into St Croix by the US Department of the Interior in Christianstad. Under the US 'New Deal' programme there was an attempt to help modernise the St Croix sugar industry, and this 1000 mm gauge locomotive probably went to the West India Sugar Factory at Bethlehem Estate, either to assist or replace the steamers, which by that time must have been well worn. Local rumour has it that this locomotive, or what remained of it, went to South America with the Bethlehem factory.

In 1904 a proposal was made to the Danish Government for a railway to connect the two main towns of Frederikstad and Christiansted. Although an engineering survey was carried out, funds were not granted by the Danish Government and nothing more happened.

The sugar factories at La Grange and Bethlehem are now little more than memories, and apart from a small length of rail preserved at Estate Whim Plantation and Museum, and some concrete telegraph posts in the middle of a field off Centerline Road, little remains of these two interesting little railways.

St Kitts

St Kitts is a long, narrow volcanic island, with a mountainous range which runs like a spine through the north part of the island. Gentle slopes, formed as the Caribbean Sea retreated during the ice age, provide the fertile cane fields through which the St Kitts Sugar Manufacturing Corporation's narrow gauge cane railway continues to wend its way.

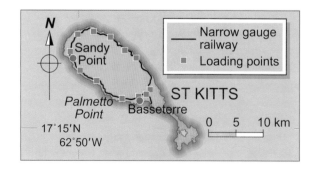

An afternoon scene in the marshalling yard at the St Kitts sugar factory as loaded trains are moved towards the mill and empty cars are prepared for another trip to the country for loading, March 1998. (Author's collection)

Each of the numerous ruined windmill towers now dotting the landscape of St Kitts marks the location of an abandoned small and self-contained sugar plantation, many of which had been converted to steam power by the 1880s. In an attempt to make the island's sugar business more competitive in the face of extended global competition, a state-of-the-art steam-powered factory was erected at Kit Stoddart's estate near Basseterre, the island's capital, in 1912. Estate owners sold their sugar cane to the new factory, rather than process it on their own estates; the factory producing a high quality sugar that was more saleable to overseas refiners. The current narrow gauge railway, laid down at the time of factory construction, was introduced to facilitate the transport of harvested cane from field to factory.

The railway began its operating life before the opening of the factory, as a short line was laid from the old dock in the centre of Basseterre out to the factory site at Kit Stoddart's, approximately a mile away. The materials required to build the factory shell, the two massive horizontal steam engines used to drive the cane mills and the processing equipment, all from Great Britain, were hauled from the pier to the factory site by a small, petrol-engined, contractor's locomotive. Concurrent with factory construction, two, 2 ft 6 in gauge lines were built. One ran east from the central marshalling yard to Christ Church, a distance of about seven miles, while the west side line skirted Basseterre, terminating at Palmetto Point about four miles away. By the time the factory opened for production in the crop season of 1912, there were almost 12 miles of single track laid through the country, transfer points and an extensive marshalling yard to the east of the factory. In 1922 water transport for cut canes was tried from Sandy Point and Middle Island, but this was unsuccessful and the railway was extended to Sandy Point for the 1923 crop.

By 1926 the success of the factory and railway was assured, and, in conjunction with expansion at the factory, the two lines were connected through to Dieppe Bay at the north of the island to form a

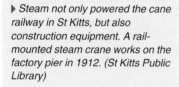

continuous circle. Simultaneously, the opportunity was taken to install a number of passing loops and transfer sidings, and to increase the track length to almost 30 miles.

The volcanic origins of St Kitts, while providing many spectacular vistas along the track route, made for a difficult place to build a railway. The many deep ravines bisecting the undulating cane-growing areas necessitated a number of expensive bridges, and frequent tropical storms causing severe washouts continue to make track maintenance a costly business. Little or no ballast is used; the track being laid directly onto the ground. Drainage construction was minimal, even in cuttings that are most liable to flooding, and while some improvements have been introduced,

erosion remains a problem on some parts of the track. Originally laid with 30lb rail spiked to steel trough sleepers, much of the main line has now been upgraded to 35lb rail. While in some areas the track is almost at sea level, in other parts of the island it follows the 100 ft level contour. The average grade throughout the system is 1 in 100, with three degree curves, making the system well within the capabilities of the current locomotives. The 26 bridges used to cross the numerous ravines range in size from a nondescript seven footer to a spectacular 360 ft girder bridge that crosses the island's main road on the east coast.

Initial operating motive power was supplied by a fleet of four 0-4-2ST Kerr, Stuart *Brazil* class steam locomotives. This original stable was augmented by three additional locomotives of the same class, one delivered in 1916 and two in July of 1922. With their 9 in x 15 in cylinders and light weight-to-power ratio, these popular locomotives did very well handling heavily-laden trains on the lightly laid track. With the exception of one, all the steam locomotives were scrapped on-site by 1972.

Motive power on the system now comprises 19 operating locomotives. The oldest, an Armstrong Whitworth from 1934, pulls tanker cars of molasses to the harbour, a duty it has carried out since being commissioned. Main line duties are shared between the stable of seven Hunslet DMs, eight Rustons (six 100DLs and two 48DLs), the six DLs coming from the Antigua Gunthorpes railway system which was abandoned in 1974. In addition, Whitcombes, Davenports, Plymouths and Motor Rails (some from the First World War era) have been used on the system. A number of the railway's current locomotives have been re-engined over the years and several of the Rustons have recently been rebuilt in England, with good results. All main line working is done in

conjunction with a small tender, carrying water for ballast, and sand to assist with braking and traction.

As with many supposedly inanimate objects, locomotives often seem to have a life (or mind) of their own. On the St Kitts system, one of the two Davenport 0-6-0 connecting rod drive engines was given the name *Churchill*, because when carrying road No. 13 it seemed to have a propensity to find accidents or derail at the slightest provocation. Since the change it seems to have behaved itself! Ruston-built locomotive No. 4 began to display the same anti-social tendencies, being involved in a number of accidents over the years, rolling onto its side on one occasion and finally derailing in front of the Controller's Tower at the factory. Based on previous successfully applied locomotive psychology, in 1989 a No.1 was added to the locomotive number, with the result that there are now two No. 14s running, and the anti-social nature of former Ruston No. 4 seems to have been cured!

Hand or machine-cut cane is now taken to the loading, or transfer points, in trailers drawn by tractor. Trains of empty cane cars are placed on transfer sidings at each loading point, and rather ancient Jones cranes sling each trailer load of cane into a cane car. Locomotives haul rakes of empty cars from the marshalling yard at the factory to the various loading points, returning with a train of full wagons to the factory. In the factory marshalling yard the full wagons are pushed over the weigh bridge by the yard engines then moved to the mill loading area, where they are mechanically tipped. The factory requires over 2500 tons of cane per day for efficient operation. With maximum train size being about 80 tons, it can be seen that the railway department has its work cut out in order to provide a non-stop flow of cane to the mills. They have resorted to some night running in recent years, in order to maintain a full flow of cane for the mill.

Ruston and Hornsby 0-6-0 diesel mechanical locomotive, and in the background, a larger Hunslet, keep company in the yard at the St Kitt's Sugar Factory, April 1998. (Author's collection)

In a scene repeated today at harvest time, albeit with a diesel locomotive in charge, a loaded train crosses the St Kitts island main road near Nicola Town on its way to the factory. (Brimstone Hill Fortress National Park Society)

Derailing cane cars and the heavy traffic carried means that ongoing and annual track maintenance is necessary. Major track repair work is carried out when the factory is closed. Each weekday two or three maintenance trains leave the main yard to travel east and west, in order to carry out track realignment, rail replacement and maintenance; the trains and crews returning late afternoon to the marshalling yard at the factory. On occasions a large bulldozer is transported on a small flat-bed truck, dwarfing not only the truck but also the locomotive! The cost of track maintenance alone is about EC$2 million per year (US$750,000). While the railway is currently an effective means of transporting a large volume of cane to the factory, its annual maintenance cost and the cost of its large seasonal and full-time operating staff is a heavy burden on an industry currently struggling for economic survival.

The St Kitts cane railway continues to hang on to life after 80 years of operation, in spite of hurricanes, tropical storms and years of inadequate funds to provide for essential maintenance. Operating year after year through the dedication of its maintenance staff and operating crews, the railway makes a vital contribution to the island's sugar industry, and also provides visitors to this spectacular island with a unique added attraction. A tourist train was tried years ago, and while popular with visitors, its winter-time operation conflicted with the efficient movement of cane to the factory. In the future, however, this could be less of a problem, given the present efficient management of the system and a consolidation of cane lands into one part of the island. Perhaps one day a refurbished *Brazil* class steam locomotive will again be seen meandering its way across the Wingfield River bridge to the delight of visitors and Kittitians' young and old.

Safety and efficient operation are of primary concern to the system managers, and to this end block system running is carried out, with all locomotives and loading points in VHF radio contact with the Traffic Control Office at Kit Stoddart's. Permission has to be obtained from the Traffic Office for a locomotive and train to enter a block. Signalmen are also in VHF contact with Traffic Control. Stationing a locomotive at the north end of the island to move trains to points on the east or west coast for collection by locos from the factory has also simplified cane transfer and line operation. The island main road and the railway often share the same areas of flat land, and a feature of driving around the island during the winter harvest time are the numerous manned crossing gates.

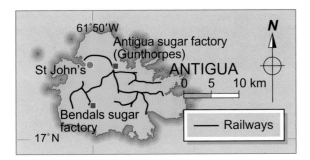

ANTIGUA

Reputedly having a beach for each day of the year, Antigua lies at the heart of the Caribbean, almost equidistant from Florida and Venezuela. A low-lying coral island, with intermittent rainfall, Antigua nevertheless produced cane sugar from the mid-1600s until 1971, when a political decision was made to abandon the industry completely and concentrate on tourism.

Antigua is a relatively flat island, which, while not conducive to promoting rainfall, was an advantage when it came to building cane railways to supply the two factories built on the island in the early part of the twentieth century.

The Antigua Central Factory

In common with the other Caribbean cane sugar producers, Antigua developed a plantation system of small estates, each processing its own cane. As on many islands, the remains of these estates, in the form of windmill towers and boiling houses, can be seen dotted around the countryside.

After many years of unsure markets and global competition, the sugar industry on the English colonial islands in the Caribbean gained some reprieve with the allocation of sugar quotas in 1901. On Antigua the

result of this boost in fortunes resulted in the construction of two privately-owned new Central factories, one at Gunthorpe's Estate to the east of St John's, the island's capital, and another at Bendals to the south of St Johns. Both factories were located on the flat, fertile parts of the island. As with the St Kitt's factory, construction was made possible with financial assistance from the British Government. The new factory, known officially as the Antigua Sugar Factory (but often locally as 'Gunthorpes'), opened in 1905 and processed over 1600 tons of cane that year. The factory was expanded in 1910, with the tonnage of processed cane increasing dramatically over the next few years, with a crop of 70,349 tons of cane producing over 7000 tons of sugar in 1913. By 1915 there was very little of the old style muscavado sugar being produced on the island.

Contemporary with factory construction, a railway right-of-way of surprising length had been laid through the central part of Antigua. The Gunthorpes railway, of 2 ft 6 in gauge, eventually extended north and west from the factory to Point Wharf in St John's, south and west towards Bendals and south-east to Little Duers, now the site of Potworks Dam and reservoir. In all there were almost 50 miles of single track attached to the factory. Originally laid using hardwood sleepers imported from British Guiana, the change was later made to pressed metal sleepers imported from England. The railway was expanded a number of times in order to provide a better service to cane growers.

The initial locomotives on the Gunthorpes line were two of the very popular Kerr, Stuart *Tattoo* class 0-4-0 saddle tanks, named *Sir Neville Lubbock* and *Sir Gerald Strickland*. As factory output expanded, and more cane needed to be moved from the field to the mill, seven additional locomotives were purchased, this time Kerr, Stuart *Brazil* class 0-4-2 saddle tanks. Apparently three of the *Brazil* class locomotives were

built for oil firing, probably as a result of concerns about lineside fires, although coal was the fuel generally used. The locomotive crew consisted of a driver, a breakman and a couple of 'pointboys', who were charged with point changes and general assistance as the train was assembled and moved through the system to the factory yard.

The largest locomotive in the Gunthorpe fleet was No. 7, *Joan*, a Kerr, Stuart 0-6-2 *Matary* class tank engine. The last of its type to be built, the engine was fitted with a larger *Huxley* class boiler. Delivered in 1927, this powerful engine was perhaps too much for the lightly-laid and poorly-maintained track, but she survived until 1971, when she was repatriated to the Welshpool & Llanfair Railway in Wales for use on this tourist line.

In addition to its steam locomotives, the Antigua Sugar Factory railway managed to accumulate a collection of petrol-engined locomotives. In the early 1920s a number of rebuilt First World War Simplex locomotives, which had reputedly seen service on the front lines, were added to the locomotive fleet, later to be joined by three Plymouths and a 1946 loco from the Vulcan Iron Works in the United States. Commencing in 1954, the railway went through a period of upgrading and modernisation, with a number of Ruston and Hornsby 100DL 0-6-0 diesel mechanical locomotives being brought in to replace the ageing mixture of steam and petrol-engined locomotives. By 1970 the track serving the Gunthorpes factory had been reduced to about 30 miles in length, with the harvested cane being hauled to the mill in Hudson or Gregg cane cars (known as 'bagoons' on the island), by the diesel locomotives.

Steam did not disappear completely on the Antigua Sugar Factory railway with the introduction of the diesel fleet. In 1968, *Brazil* class locomotive *George* was given a snappy blue and silver livery and had the name *Sunshine Shu-Shu* painted on its saddle tank. Thus transformed from work-a-day locomotive to tourist attraction, *George* ran a short train of converted cane cars during the winter tourist season on part of the sugar factory line. Sadly, this second life for the Antigua Sugar Factory railway did not work out, and once again *George* was relegated to the out-of-service line.

The six Antigua Ruston & Hornsby 100DL diesel locomotives went to the sugar factory on St Kitts when the Antigua railway closed.

Bendals sugar factory

At the smaller Bendals factory, built in 1903-4, almost 10 miles of 2 ft 0 in gauge track was laid. Two small plantation-style 0-6-0 Orenstein & Koppel steam locomotives (*Thistle* and *Rose*) might well have been the originals for the railway. They were later joined by two Plymouth 0-4-0 petrol mechanical locomotives built in 1918-19.

In 1926 the Gunthorpes railway was extended to Bendals in order to allow for the transfer of cane when the Gunthorpes factory was overloaded. Some of the Bendals system was converted to 2 ft 6 in gauge when, after another long period of depression in the sugar industry, operation of the smaller factory was taken over by Gunthorpes in 1936. As three derelict Plymouths remain in Antigua and only one was known to have been ordered for the Gunthorpes factory, those from the Bendals factory were most likely re-gauged and pressed into service. The Bendals railway finally closed in 1958.

Labour problems, a disastrous drought in the 1960s, and a glutted sugar market combined with the increasing role of tourism in Antigua, saw the

production of cane sugar, and the Gunthorpe's railway, abandoned in 1971 by the Antigua Government, the final owners of the factories.

GUADELOUPE

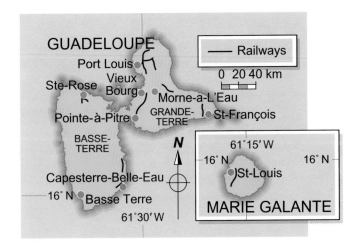

A *departement* of France, Guadeloupe is the most southerly of the Leewards, comprising two islands, Basse-Terre and Grande-Terre, separated by a narrow river. A third smaller island, Marie-Galante, lies to the south of Grande-Terre. While Grande-Terre and Marie-Galante are generally flat, Basse-Terre has a considerable mountain range. Today, the manufacture of *rhum* and some sugar provides a market for the decreasing acreage of sugar cane still grown on the island.

After 1720 the acreage planted to sugar cane on Guadeloupe grew substantially, until it became the main agricultural crop. The industry closely followed the pattern found on other large Caribbean islands, and by the late 1840s, after the devastation of the 1843 earthquake and emancipation in 1848, small owner-operated sugar factories began to be replaced by steam-powered Centrals, or usines, and by the late 1860s there were ten in operation. Apart from two on the southern, flatter end of Basse-Terre, and two on Marie-Galante, the other new factories were on Grande-Terre. About 40,000 tons of sugar were being produced on the island in the late 1890s and growth in the industry, especially in the face of stiff competition provided to cane sugar by French-grown beet sugar, ensured the further centralisation of cane sugar production and investment in larger Centrals. It was this further centralisation of cane processing that precipitated the railways of Guadeloupe.

On the island of Grande-Terre sugar manufacturing eventually concentrated on three areas; to the north of Pointe-à-Pitre, the main city on the island, on the Plaine de la Simonière in the east, and in the area of Beauport in the north of the island. While the sugar factories often used British machinery, the cane railways invariably chose to support European locomotive builders.

Probably the largest rail system on Guadeloupe was at the Usine de Beauport, an extensive 1200 mm gauge network that ran to the north, east and south of the factory, with a rail connection to the sea, possibly at Port-Louis. The Usine Darboussier, on the southern outskirts of Pointe-à-Pitre, had a standard gauge railway network that headed north-east of the city, and on towards Vieux-Bourg and Morne-à-l'Eau. The third railway network on Grande-Terre served the factories on the flat plain north of the coastal town of St-François. This area, known as the Plaine de la Simonière, was ideally suited for cane cultivation and for railway operation. The line ran east-west with a short north line to Gardel.

In addition to the standard gauge and 1200 mm systems, lines of 1000, 750, 600 and 500 mm. were used. A variety of locomotives, both steam and diesel, operated on the various networks. Early steam locomotives from such well-known French builders as Corpet Louvet and Decauville operated along with products of the German builders, Krauss and Borsig. Other European manufacturers such as Cail, St Leonard and Couillet also supplied steam locomotives to Guadeloupe in the latter years of the nineteenth century.

The locomotives of Corpet Louvet were popular in both Guadeloupe and Martinique. Of the locomotives built by the company during almost a century of production, the majority were 0-6-0 narrow gauge tank engines, many of these finding their way to the sugar mills and mines in French colonial possessions. Established in 1855, the company became Corpet Louvet in 1912 on moving to a large factory near Paris.

While unusual looking, the Brown valve gear fitted to this 1925 Corpet Louvet locomotive proved popular. Many similar locomotives were used on cane railways in Guadeloupe and Martinique. (K.W. Clingan)

Their first narrow gauge locomotive, an 0-4-0 tank, was supplied to Martinique in 1869, the first of many to the French Caribbean. In 1880 Corpet Louvet began to use Brown valve gear, a design that incorporated an intermediate rocker arm that took the movement of the piston rod to the connecting rod. Narrow gauge locomotives fitted with the Brown valve gear were popular on cane railways, given the gear's simplicity, massive proportions and location high up on the frames where it was well away from dust and abrasive soil. The last Corpet Louvet locomotive was probably delivered to the island in 1927, one of the ubiquitous 0-6-0 tank engines for 1200 mm gauge.

Another large supplier of locomotives to Guadeloupe sugar estates was Decauville. The gauge of the numerous 0-4-0s and 0-6-0s supplied to the island from 1880 to 1913 varied from 500 mm to 750 mm, indicating that these were light locomotives most likely used in conjunction with the company's patented portable or semi-portable track. Of interest amongst the locomotives supplied to Guadeloupe, and attributed to Decauville (but built by the Belgian company Les Ateliers Matallurgiques Nivelles, and known as 'Turbize'), was a 600 mm 0-4-4-0 Mallet tank supplied in 1889. These powerful little locomotives were popular in Europe, their flexibility and light axle loading making them ideal for lightly-laid lines. No doubt these attributes outweighed the added complication and maintenance of the two sets of cylinders and valve gear used.

The large Usine Darboussier accepted cane both from barges brought alongside the factory and from its standard gauge railway. Three 0-4-0 Cail tank locomotives from the late 1860s, and an 0-6-0 Krauss tank engine (one of five supplied to Guadeloupe, the others being used on the Beauport system) worked on the factory railway.

On Basse-Terre only the terrain in the north-east and along the south-east coast is suitable for growing sugar cane. In 1875 and 1880 two usines were built in the south of the island at Bologne (Basse-Terre) and Marquisat (Capesterre) respectively. At a later date a further factory was built in the north east in the Ste Rose area. Locomotives built by Decauville and Krauss were used on Basse-Terre

On the island of Marie Galante Central factories opened in the 1860s. A 500 mm railway, using a Decauville 0-4-0 tank, supplied in 1893, served one of the island's Centrals, most probably the one now known as Grande-Anse, located on the west coast and to the south of St Louis, the island's main settlement.

Retrenchment of the cane sugar industry in the French islands after the Second World War saw an expansion in production, with 79,000 tons of sugar exported in 1951 as opposed to only 54,000 tons in 1939. In 1953, 12 mills were in operation. Modernisation of the railways saw a number of Brookville 4-and 6-wheel diesel mechanical locomotives imported into the island, and at the same time there appears to have been a substantial contraction in the rail system, as trucks were readily available and the road system improved, offering a more economical and flexible way of transporting cane.

There was some rail activity in the 1970s on Guadeloupe, and even later on Marie-Galante. Ox carts, trucks and tractor-drawn trailers now provide cane transport to the numerous small distilleries that continue to operate on all three islands. The large factory at Pointe-à-Pitre, once at the hub of a substantial narrow gauge railway, remains as a rusted wreck waiting for possible conversion into a marina.

Chapter 9

Windward Islands: Dominica, Martinique and St Lucia

DOMINICA

The most northerly of the Windward islands, the Commonwealth of Dominica remains a rugged, mountainous island covered with large areas of tropical forest. Sugar cane growing was only partially successful, as there was insufficient flat land to make the industry viable. However, timber harvesting has been carried out on the island intermittently since before European colonisation, and it was timber, rather than sugar, that inspired the island's first and only railway.

In an effort to increase settlement in Dominica, a circular was produced in 1903 by the colonial administration. Note was made in the circular regarding the extensive timber stands remaining untapped on the island. In 1909 further efforts were carried out to try to develop the island's timber industry and it is in this context that the first mention is made of a light railway to be used to bring timber to the coast.

Eventually the timber concessions offered by the Colonial Government were taken up, and The Forest Timber Company was established to harvest timber growing in the interior of the island. The next business noted as being involved with timber harvesting on Dominica is the Dominica Forest Ltd at Portsmouth in

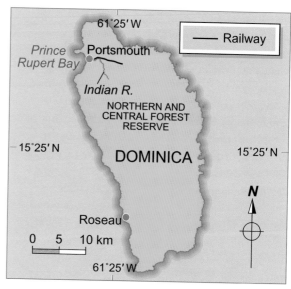

the north of the island. Their assets were acquired by the Dominica Forests and Sawmills Ltd in December of 1910. The railway was in operation by then, as Forests and Sawmills Ltd were to purchase not only the forest, but also the railway of their predecessor.

Logging was carried out inland from Portsmouth, which lies at the mouth of the Indian River. The railway would have followed the river valley into the forest, probably following the line that is now the highway. The railway was of 3 ft 0 in gauge and used one of Kerr, Stuart's ubiquitous *Brazil* class 0-4-2 tank

The sole locomotive on the Dominic Forest Ltd railway, a Kerr, Stuart Brazil class 0-4-2 tank locomotive, on the company's logging line c.1910. (Author's collection)

locomotives of 1910. It is thought the railway, along with the sawmills, was abandoned about 1914, the site eventually becoming used for the packing of bananas.

MARTINIQUE

While somewhat smaller than its sister island Guadeloupe, Martinique is also an island with mountains and plains. Blessed with fertile soils and adequate rainfall, sugar cane cultivation was, and remains, a major industry on the island.

The pattern of Central factory development closely followed that of Guadeloupe, and the first of Martinique's Centrals opened under English ownership in 1868. Located at Fort-de-France, the island's capital, the factory was able to accept cane

Fitted with conventional valve gear, this narrow gauge Corpet Louvet 0-6-0 locomotive is preserved at the rum museum in Martinique. (Author's collection)

railways to one extent or other. None of the lines were particularly long, as the factories tended to be in small plains surrounded by mountains, thus limiting the area where cane could be grown. The longest system, which was probably Lamentin, was reported as having 21 miles of track, six 0-6-0 Corpet Louvet locomotives and about 170 six to ten-ton capacity cane cars.

Locomotive imports followed a somewhat different pattern to that found in Guadeloupe. In the early 1870s Corpet Louvet locomotives began to appear in number on the island, although more correctly these locomotives should be called Corpet, as the 'Louvet' did not appear on builder's plates until the 1890s. Many of the locomotives imported were 0-4-0 tank engines of various gauges from 1280 mm down to 1160 mm gauge and they were widely distributed throughout the various railway systems. In the late 1800s and early 1900s the larger Corpet Louvet 0-6-0 tank engines were introduced, again widely distributed. In total, 33 locomotives from this manufacturer worked on Martinique, and the island has the distinction of taking the first and last of a long list of narrow gauge locomotives built by the company. The first, named *La Perle*, (a 1200 mm 0-4-0 tank) was delivered to the Usine de la Dillon in 1870 and the last one (a 1160 mm gauge 0-6-0 tank locomotive fitted with Brown valve gear) went to the Usine Bassignac in 1931.

Two Vulcan Ironworks 0-6-0 tank locomotives went to Martinique during the First World War, no doubt as a result of shortages in France, and two Cail 1280 mm 0-4-0 tank locomotives and a 1280 mm 0-6-0 Decauville were also used on the island's cane railways.

Just prior to and immediately after the Second World War diesel locomotives were introduced to Martinique. A number of Brookville, Davenport and Whitcomb 4wDM and 6wDM locomotives replaced a

shipped by sea and land. By 1885 fourteen more *usines* had been built. With the selling price of sugar continuing to decline towards the end of the nineteenth century, factories were forced to become more efficient and produce more sugar each harvest. More sugar production meant that more cane needed to be hauled to the factory from further afield, and there became the rationale for the introduction of cane railways on Martinique. This was obviously quite a different situation from St Kitts and Antigua, where the railway was built as an integral part of the new Central factory and not added afterwards as production warranted.

From the list of locomotives imported into the island, it is possible to piece together some of the early history of cane railways on Martinique. There were in total 13 factories that have been identified as using

number of the very old, and no doubt by that time well worn, steam locomotives.

With the exception of Usine Galion, today's working sugar mills in Martinique produce cane juice for processing into rum. Apart from two preserved locomotives and some railway bridge remains, there are now very few vestiges of the various cane railways once to be found on the island.

ST LUCIA

St Lucia has limited flat land, restricting the cultivation of sugar cane to coastal areas. While cane is still grown on the island for the production of rum, the sugar industry on the island ended in the early 1960s. Bananas are now the main agricultural crop.

The Central Factory (Cul de Sac Co. Ltd) in Cul de Sac Valley, to the south of Port Castries, was reported to be operating a 13-mile-long narrow gauge railway, using three diesel locomotives and over 130 steel cane cars in the mid-1950s. Two Plymouth 4wPM locomotives had been supplied to the factory in 1927-8. The line supposedly used wood-burning steam locomotives, of undetermined make, in the 1920s.

The Roseau factory, in the Roseau Valley about seven miles south of Castries, had about 1000 acres of sugar cane under cultivation in the mid-1950s. The factory was reported to have in operation at that time a narrow gauge railway 16 miles in length, with three diesel locomotives and 145 cane cars. Again, wood-burning steam locomotives were the original motive power on the railway, and it is not known when the change to diesels took place. The Roseau factory is now the home for St Lucia Distillers Ltd, but prior to this was the centre for the extensive banana operations conducted by Geest Industries. The company utilised

an extensive railway system (mostly the remains of the old sugar railway) to transport bananas from the fields to a central packing shed. The 2 ft 8 in line used two Motor Rail, one Ruston & Hornsby and one Hibberd locomotive.

There had been two other sugar factories on St Lucia, one at Vieux Fort, near the new international airport, and one at Dennery, in the Maboya valley on the island's east coast. A 3 ft 9 in gauge Kerr, Stuart 0-4-2 tank locomotive of the *Skylark* class was supplied to Dennery & Co. in 1900, and this was probably the railway's second locomotive, the first being supplied by Fives-Lille of France.

Vieux Fort Sugar Estate operated a 1939 Vulcan ironworks 4wDM and probably, earlier, a Hartley, Arnoux & Fanning 0-4-0 tank built in 1891.

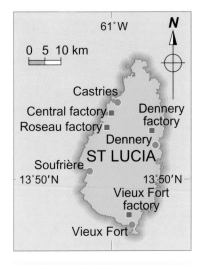

A cane train at the Roseau sugar factory, St Lucia, c.1955. (Colonial Office)

Chapter 10

Barbados

Located at the southern end of the Caribbean chain, Barbados is an island of contrasting urban sprawl and cane fields. First settled by English colonists in 1627, this limestone island gained political independence in 1966. The island is said to be the most 'English' of the Caribbean islands, with the landscape and culture lending credence to this comparison.

The growing of sugar cane came early to Barbados, and the affluence resulting from the production of sugar, rum and molasses is reflected in the wealth of colonial architectural and historic remains to be found dotted throughout the island. Over the years sugar production has been replaced as the major industry in Barbados, but despite the growth of tourism and manufacturing, a substantial crop of cane is harvested each year and processed into sugar, molasses and rum.

The Barbados General Railway

The Barbados General Railway, the Barbados Railway Company, the Bridgetown & St Andrews Railway Ltd, the Barbados Light Railway Co. Ltd and, finally, the Barbados Government Railway tried, with varying degrees of success, to operate a public railway on the island.

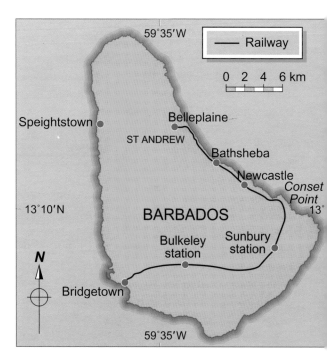

Barbados has always been densely populated, with the topography of the island encouraging settlement in the flatter, more fertile, southern half. A population density of 700 persons per square mile had been reached by 1845, prompting a Mr Simmonds, editor of the *Colonial Magazine*, to begin agitating for the

construction of a public railway. In July 1846 the Act necessary to establish the railway was passed and given the assent of the Governor, Sir Charles Grey, who by all accounts seemed to be more than a little enthusiastic about the potential for such a transport system on the island. Indeed, he felt that 'under honest, economical and prudent management the experiment would succeed, and must lead to the formation of three or four other branches, with which the whole interior and general surface of the island would be connected by inclined planes or tram-ways.' Unfortunately, the Governor's hope for prudent management and an extensive service was never to transpire during the lifetime of a railway that was lucky to make it to the far side of the island with a single track!

The original Act had been for a railway from Bridgetown, the island capital, to Speightstown, an important port approximately a dozen miles north. The railway, to be called 'The Barbados General Railway', was to be somewhere between 4 ft 6 in and 5 ft 6 in gauge and construction would be initiated when 10 per cent of the estimated £300,000 sterling cost was raised. Only £11,000 was raised, thereby ending the hopes of Barbados' first railway.

In 1873 the idea of a railway was again broached, and a number of prominent citizens of the island provided financial support for the project. However, this time the railway was to be a standard gauge line that would go from Bridgetown to St Andrews (Belleplaine) on the north-west side of the island, passing through the flat, fertile, and heavily-populated southern plains and then wending its way through the hilly Scotland district. Robert Fairlie, light railway engineer and designer of the locomotive type bearing his name, visited Barbados and made a number of recommendations on the layout of the line, all of which, with the exception of the suggestion that the

gauge should be a more sensible and economic 3 ft 6 in, seemed to have been ignored. Money was raised in England, a Board of Directors was established, and in June 1877 the first sod was turned at Newcastle. Financing was not completed at this time, so it was not until May 1879 that the construction contract was signed. In early 1881 a foreman and driver arrived from England, and a Mr Grundy, formerly of the Great Western Railway in England, arrived to take up the position of manager.

Mr Grundy succumbed to yellow fever and never saw the opening of the railway from Bridgetown to Carrington, a distance of nine miles, in October 1881. While the opening appears to have been a great social success, a passenger car derailed on the first day; more work being evidently required on the track. By December all seemed well, with regular services commencing to Carrington, less than half of the distance to the proposed terminal at Belleplaine. Land acquisition seemed to take more time than anticipated, and it was not until August 1883 that the local paper could report that a party of gentlemen had travelled all the way to Belleplaine by train. It appeared that 'The Barbados Railway Company' was finally in action! However successful the initial run, problems were encountered at Conset (where Coddrington College is now located), which was soon to become the nemesis of the railway, given the staggering 1 in 33 grade! The steepest grade in use in England is the 1 in 37 Lickey incline, and Conset was to become an ongoing operating problem, with trains often having to be divided and hauled up in two sections in order to make the ascent. Going down was obviously not to be taken lightly either, as Company Rules and Regulations insisted drivers and guards must 'have their trains well under control' on the Conset incline.

The carriage of sugar cane to the factories along the southern part of the line contributed substantially

A Barbados train in about 1925. (Edward Stoute collection, compliments of The Barbados National Trust)

towards the railway's revenue, with freight traffic income reaching an all-time high in 1890. However, the railway was expensive to operate. Corrosion of the west line from the effects of the sea air and the need for continuous maintenance resulting from the line's light construction began to eat into company profits. As no allowance had been made for depreciation, money had to be borrowed in order to effect repairs and replacement, a problem that plagued the line during its various ownerships.

In 1896 a petition for the voluntary winding up of 'The Barbados General Railway' was put before the Barbados House of Assembly. The petition was rejected, and a full inspection of the line was carried out by the owners' representative, Mr E. R. Calthrop, a very experienced railway engineer with practical knowledge of narrow gauge railway operation. Mr Calthrop was less than complementary about the railway, making a number of wide-ranging recommendations, including the reduction of gauge from the original 3 ft 6 in to 2 ft 6 in and the centralisation of sugar cane processing at only two or three factories, with branch lines to bring in cane from outlying estates. His 'downsizing' proposals were not accepted by the owners. The company was sold in 1898 to the bond holders, who, obviously not having had enough, promptly formed 'The Bridgetown and St Andrews Railway Ltd'.

The Barbados Government Railway

By 1899 service had resumed, this time on a 2 ft 6 in gauge track, with a stable of new locomotives from Baldwin in the United States and a rake of bogie cars converted from the original 4-wheel stock by the railway shops. Even these efforts were doomed. After only six years of operation, all in the red, the company went into voluntary liquidation in 1903. A new company, 'The Barbados Light Railway Co. Ltd', this time with a Government subsidy, was formed in 1905 and a new operating timetable was introduced. The 24-mile journey to Bellepaine took all of two hours. There were 13 scheduled station stops along the route and numerous 'halts' where trains could be flagged down. During the 'season' non-stop tourist trains were scheduled out to the Atlantic coast by Bathsheba.

The changes were to no avail, and the railway was taken over by the Barbados Government in 1915, to become 'The Barbados Government Railway'. Operating conditions did not improve under this new regime, and a much reduced Barbados railway closed in 1937, despite a last ditch effort in the House to save it, with a motion by the Chairman of the Railway Board that £32,000 should be allocated 'to give the people of this island a diesel-engined passenger railway service'. By the end of 1938 little remained of the railway, other than some earthworks, the Conset cutting and the Bridgetown station, which eventually became the bus station. A sad conclusion to the dreams of Sir Charles Grey.

Motive power in Barbados

Both English and American locomotives were used at various times on the Barbados railway. The original locomotive stable for the Barbados General Railway consisted of the contractor's engine, an English-built 0-4-0 saddle tank named *St Michael* (presumably after one of the parishes on Barbados), with main line operation being carried out by two 2-4-0 Avonside tender locomotives and two Vulcan Foundry 2-6-2 tank locomotives named *St George* and *Christchurch*, again after parishes on the island. With balloon stacks and open-backed cabs, these engines epitomised narrow gauge steam power. The original engines were coal fired. Two six-coupled engines by Bagnall, of England, were added to the fleet in 1891, much to the dismay of the permanent-way maintenance gang, who already had their work cut out for them given the permanently poor quality of the track. While not much heavier than the earlier engines, the Bagnalls had a very short wheel base, and soon caused havoc to the light-weight, poorly-aligned and tight-curved track. Local reports have these two locomotives eventually going to the 3 ft 6 in gauge West Coast Railway in British Guiana.

The gauge reduction in 1898 necessitated a change in motive power with four powerful American Baldwin engines being purchased. The new fleet consisted of *Alice* and *Beatrice*, 2-8-2 tank engines and *Dorothy*, a 2-6-0 tank engine. *Catherine*, an 0-6-0 tank, joined the fleet in 1920. This last engine was oil-fired, the others being converted from coal to oil at the same time. All the Baldwins lasted until the end of the railway, albeit with only two of them in operating condition. When no buyer was found for them at the disposal sale, they were cut up in the railway yard.

In the early 1930s a consultant had recommended scrapping the steam locomotives in favour of diesels, but this practical advice was not acted upon. Whether it would have saved the railway is now a moot point. In the 1937 post-closure equipment disposal notice, coach No. 16 was noted as being the 'Original m. coach', and was said to be 'serviceable' but the engine was out. This coach was most likely the remains of a 1924 Drewry car similar to those supplied to the Bermuda Railway. Ironically, before delivery to Barbados, this 60 hp 45-seater bogie rail car had been tried out on the Leek & Manifold Valley Light Railway, in England. It was on this railway that our old friend E. R. Calthrop put into practice many of his theories on the operation of a narrow gauge public railway!

The English-built 0-4-0 saddle tank named St Michael *crossing a bridge in Barbados c.1925. (Edward Stoute collection compliments of the Barbados National Trust)*

Chapter 11

Trinidad

Only seven miles off the coast of South America, and consisting of a series of mountain ranges and plains, Trinidad was properly colonised by the Spanish as late as 1783, when the Spanish King, heeding the advice of a French planter, offered free land grants to any Roman Catholics who were citizens of any country at that time friendly to Spain. As the result of this Royal Decree, the island quickly became populated and a sugar-based economy established. Trinidad became a British colony in 1797. The island, at 1860 square miles, is fairly large by Caribbean standards and now boasts a diverse economy based on petroleum and natural gas, sugar, tourism and manufacturing.

The Trinidad Government Railway

Nineteenth-century Trinidad, in common with many of the larger Caribbean islands, had a developing sugar-based economy but very poor internal communications. Goods, agricultural produce and people travelled to the nearest port, from where small coastal sailing vessels carried them to the large population centres.

In 1839 a local planter built a mule-operated light railway from San Fernando south to the Cipero River. The river mouth had been dredged, and the area quickly became an important port for local merchants and estates. A small industrial complex was built at the port and two intermediate stations were added to the line. In 1840 the railway was extended east to the town of Mission (now known as Princes Town). In 1864 the first steam locomotive was introduced into Trinidad. Amidst great rejoicing, the locomotive *Forerunner* departed from the railway terminus at Cipero to make the 15-mile, incident-free journey to Princes Town in 40 minutes. After numerous celebratory toasts by the citizens of that town, it made a successful return journey.

The Trinidad Government Railway opened its first passenger-carrying service in July of 1876, on a line linking the island capital, Port of Spain, with the small town of Arouca. The original 12 miles of track were extended further east about a month later to Arima, which by the 1870s had become the centre of the island's expanding cocoa industry. This standard gauge line was eventually extended south to San Fernando in April of 1882, and from here a line was built to Princes Town. Other extensions and additional lines followed in due course. By 1914 the Trinidad Government Railway boasted a route length of over 107 miles, providing a popular and economical means of passenger and freight transportation for the island.

Much of the Trinidad Government Railway line was planned to pass through fertile agricultural areas,

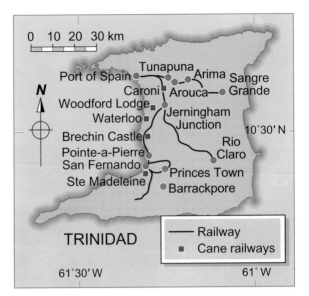

TRINIDAD

0 10 20 30 km

N

Port of Spain
Tunapuna
Arima
Sangre Grande
Caroni
Arouca
Woodford Lodge
Waterloo
Jerningham Junction
Brechin Castle
Pointe-a-Pierre
Rio Claro
San Fernando
Princes Town
Ste Madeleine
Barrackpore

10°30′ N

61°30′ W   61° W

—— Railway
■ Cane railways

Ready to go out with the permanent way gang. Photographed at Port of Spain in 1948. (G.F. Abbott collection R. R. Darsley)

and the expensive extension from Tabaquite to Rio Claro to the east of San Fernando, was approved by the Trinidad legislature in 1906, expressly to allow the opening up of over 10,000 acres of prime agricultural land in addition to providing a rail service to over 65,000 people living in the area. The railway's only tunnel was located on this branch, opening in 1898 after taking 200 workers two years to construct. Further extensions in the pre-First World War period linked San Fernando with Siparia, further to the south, providing the railway with additional business generated by the estimated population of 14,000 people and the agricultural produce from over 14,000 acres of fertile land.

The Trinidad Government Railway soon became a profitable concern. In 1881 over 705,000 fare paying passengers were carried, although income was much lower than expenditure. By the early 1900s income exceeded expenditure by a healthy margin. In 1911 the railway ran over 349,000 train miles and made an operating profit of over £22,000 sterling. In 1922 a

popular guide to the West Indies was able to inform travellers that the rail journey between Port of Spain and San Fernando was timetabled to take 1 hour and 48 minutes for the 35-mile journey, and that by far the most scenic run was that between Port of Spain and Sangre Grande, the journey offering views of the mountains and extensive cocoa plantations.

By the mid-1920s the railway was operating some 140 miles of line, including the Cipero Tramway, which it had taken over. Passenger revenues were almost three times higher than freight revenues, an unusual situation on many Caribbean railways, no doubt being the result of a large population with limited travel options and no seasonal sugar cane traffic (there were extensive cane railways on the islands, as will be seen later). However, while receipts were rising, so were expenditures, with the result that the local government was having to support the railway in a substantial manner. The railway was a relatively sophisticated operation by this time (certainly by Caribbean standards). Traffic control was by either the

▲ *The Trinidad Government Railway owned a number of these Montreal Locomotive Works' locomotives. This example was built in 1919. (Dr D. A. Down collection R. R. Darsley)*

▶ *Trinidad Government Railway Bo–Bo DE built by General Electric in 1942, photographed hauling a San Fernando Race Train in 1948. (G.F. Abbott collection R.R. Darsley)*

electric tablet system or the staff-and-pass system. Semaphore signals for 'home' and 'distant' were used at some locations, especially main line junctions and where estate lines crossed the main line.

While traffic grew, aided by the development of the Trinidad oil industry and the Second World War, there was increased competition from road transport as highways were constructed, often using the pitch harvested from the famous 'Pitch Lake' located south of San Fernando. This brought an eventual post-war decrease in traffic and an increased government subsidy for the railway.

As the result of a review of the railway operation all services on the railway, apart from the Port of Spain to Arima branch, ended in 1963. The end came for the Trinidad Government Railway in early December 1968, when the final section of line, that from St Joseph to Tunapuna, on the Arima line, closed for passenger traffic and was replaced by a bus service.

Motive power and rolling stock

Throughout its operating life the Trinidad Government Railway used a varied fleet of locomotives and rolling stock, with motive power being purchased from a number of North American and English builders.

Initial main line motive power for the railway was provided by a fleet of attractive 4-4-0 tank locomotives built by Kitson of Leeds, England. For work around the main station in Port of Spain and dock and yard work small Hunslet 0-4-0 and 0-6-0 tank locomotives were purchased. Other steam locomotives, growing in size and power over the years, were supplied to the railway by other British manufacturers such as Armstrong Whitworth, Nysmyth Wilson and Beyer Peacock.

North American locomotives made an appearance on the Trinidad Government Railway in 1919, with the arrival of a number of Montreal Locomotive Works 0-6-0 tank engines and three powerful 4-6-0 tender engines. Between 1921 and 1942 eight additional 4-6-0 tender locomotives and three 2-8-0 tender locomotives were supplied to the railway by the Montreal Locomotives Works of Montreal, Canada. With the advent of locally-produced oil, and continuing claims against the railway for track-side fires, the steam locomotives on the TGR were converted to oil firing.

A Hunslet 0-8-0 diesel mechanical locomotive was delivered in the early 1940s with nine General Electric Bo-Bo diesel electric locomotives, all from the US Army Transportation Corps, joining the railway's locomotive fleet after the war. The railway flirted with rail cars on two occasions, both with limited success. In the early 1900s two Beyer Peacock, ex- London, Brighton & South Coast Railway steam 'motor cars' were imported, but apparently never ran, and in the last part of the railway's life two ex-British Rail Wickham two-car diesel multiple units were used.

Trinidad cane railways

Trinidad possesses large areas of flat fertile land, ideal for the growing of sugar cane. By the middle of the nineteenth century many small estates had begun to amalgamate to form large Central factories, or as they were known on Trinidad, *usines* and it was this consolidation that was the catalyst for the introduction

This anonymous well tank worked at the Esperanza sugar factory. It was photographed in1956. (Dr D.A Down collection R.R. Darsley)

95

With the massive Ste Madeleine factory chimney in the background one of the factory's two working Hunslet sit at the head of a rake of empty cane cars in preparation for the afternoon trip into the countryside. (Author's collection)

of a substantial privately-owned railway system on the island.

Trinidad cane railways used standard and narrow gauge track of 2 ft 6 in, 3 ft 0 in and 3 ft 6 in gauge. Standard gauge was used at some of the factories to give direct access to the Trinidad Government Railway for the transport of bagged (and later bulk) sugar to the docks for export, the massive Usine Ste Madeleine being one example.

In 1870 sugar machinery engineers George Fletcher & Co. of Derby, England, built the Usine Ste Madeleine. Beginning in the late 1800s three Hunslet standard gauge locomotives were used, the first of many to be employed on this system that eventually extended to over 80 miles of track. Waterloo Estates, to the north of Usine Ste Madeleine, purchased two Kerr, Stuart standard gauge 0-4-2 tank locomotives in 1897 and 1898, and before the turn of the century a number of standard gauge and narrow gauge engines had been delivered to Brechin Castle Estate, Bronte

Estate and Caroni Estate by British locomotive builders.

As well as more conventional locomotives used on the cane railways, two Chaplin vertical-boilered standard gauge 0-4-0 tank engines were supplied to the Colonial Company Ltd in the early 1870s, most likely for use at Usine Ste Madeleine. An Aveling & Porter 4-wheel locomotive, of traction engine design with the cylinder on top of the boiler, was supplied to the same factory.

In the early 1900s larger locomotives began to appear on the various estate railways, with English builders continuing to be favoured. In a fit of patriotism, a number of Kerr, Stuart 0-4-2 tank engines, delivered in the opening days of the First World War to Ste Madeleine, were named after well-known English admirals and generals. In the late 1920s and early 30s three hefty and powerful Hunslet standard gauge 2-6-2 tank engines were supplied to the Ste Madeleine factory. These proved to be the last

steam locomotives added to the fleet. Brechin Castle and Caroni Estates used several ALCO 0–4–2 tank engines from the 1915-19 period.

Even while steam continued as a mainstay of the locomotive fleets at each factory (the last of the big 2–6–2 Hunslets was delivered in 1934), diesel locomotives were beginning to make in-roads on the cane railways. Commencing in 1938 Vulcan Iron Works 4-wheel and 6-wheel diesel mechanical locomotives were being delivered to several of the estates, and one of the 6-wheelers is preserved at Brechin Castle factory. By the early 1940s both Hunslet and Ruston and Hornsby were supplying diesel locomotives to various estates, the last example being a Hunslet diesel hydraulic delivered to Caroni Ltd in 1976.

Consolidation in the sugar industry in Trinidad began in the early 1920s, and by 1976 the remaining factories were owned and operated by the Trinidad and Tobago Government as Caroni (1976) Ltd with sugar being produced at Ste Madeleine, Brechin Castle and Woodford Lodge. In 1998 Ste Madeleine, Brechin Castle and Woodford Lodge were still operating but only Ste Madeleine had cane delivered by rail, with two 1950s Hunslet diesels mechanical locomotives providing the motive power to haul Gregg 12-ton capacity high-sided bogie cane cars to the factory on the standard gauge Barrackpore branch.

Road transport, using tractor trailer units, was much in evidence in the area during the 1998 crop harvest, and transport department officials at Ste Madeleine believed that 1998 would be the final season for the railway. Sadly, their prediction came true, ending over 100 years of cane railways in Trinidad, victims of high operating and maintenance costs.

Refinery railways

The world's first oil well was drilled in Trinidad in 1857, but commercial production did not begin until 1910, when 125,000 barrels of crude oil were exported. Refineries developed along the coast in the area north of San Fernando, and several small steam locomotives worked in oil fields on the island. Shell Oil operated an oil field amongst the cane fields of Barrackpore, using a 2 ft 6 in narrow gauge railway with Ruston and Hornsby diesel locomotives. The movement of tank cars to the ports for export provided a substantial business for the Trinidad Government Railway, and standard gauge sidings were common in the refineries. The later adoption of pipelines and bulk tankers rendered this railway business obsolete.

◀ Frederick *was built by ALCO at the Cooke Works in 1915 for Caroni Estates, one of Trinidad's largest sugar producers. (ALCO Historic Photos)*

▲ *Oil tanker trains were regular work for the Trinidad Government Railway. In 1945 Kitson 4-4-0 of 1895 with a non-original 6-wheel tender and extended smokebox, is seen at work near Point-à-Pierre. (Dr D.A Down collection R.R. Darsley)*

◀ *This large Hunslet 2–6–2 tank locomotive of 1934, seen here working in 1956, was based at the Usine Ste Madeleine in southern Trinidad. (Dr D.A. Down collection R.R. Darsley)*

Chapter 12

Aruba and Curaçao

The Dutch islands of Aruba, Bonaire and Curaçao, commonly known as the ABC islands, are located off the coast of Venezuela, considerably to the west of their nearest Caribbean neighbours. Formerly Spanish, the islands became Dutch colonial possessions in 1634.

While lack of adequate rainfall and poor soil prevented the development of a viable sugar cane agriculture, geology and location played an important part in the economic transformation of Aruba and Curaçao.

ARUBA

The Aruba Phosphate Company

Flat, dry Aruba seems an unlikely candidate for an extensive railway history, but mineral extraction and oil refining on this 75 square mile island initiated a flurry of narrow gauge railway activity that lasted almost 100 years, ceasing only in 1959.

Phosphate became an important commodity in the late nineteenth century. It was not only used as an agricultural fertiliser but became an important ingredient in the manufacture of matches and in other industrial processes. Large deposits of phosphate were discovered in Aruba in 1874 on the island's eastern tip,

and the Aruba Phosphate Company began work in 1879 to exploit the deposits. Interestingly, the company's charter with the Government specifically allowed it to 'buy, hire or build' railways. The steam era on Aruba was about to begin!

The Directors of the Aruba Phosphate Company Ltd soon found it was impractical to move large quantities of bulky material by donkey cart from the mine area to the harbour at Sint Nicolaas, on the island's south-eastern shore. By the end of 1881 a new four-mile long 2 ft 0 in gauge railway connected the mines at Cerroe Colorada and Cerroe Culebra with a new pier at Sint Nicolaas.

Full trains ran down an incline to the dock, making easy work for the locomotive. Once the ore was tipped into the holds of ocean-going ships, the empty wagons were hauled back up the grade by the locomotive, ready to be spotted at the shafts for re-filling. Traffic

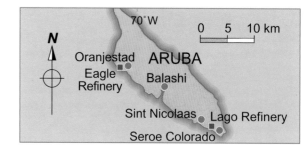

was sufficient to warrant the purchase of a second locomotive, of unknown make but believed to be an English 0-4-0 like the first locomotive. In 1882 a third steam locomotive, this time from America, was delivered to the mine. This H.K. Porter 0-4-2 tank engine was able to haul 20 or so loaded wagons each trip, with as much as 300 tons of phosphate ore being mined, transported to the dock and loaded each day.

The discovery of vast phosphate deposits in North America and North Africa spelled the end for the Aruba Phosphate Company. While it hung on through the early 1900s, by the outbreak of the First World War it became impossible to ship the ore, and the mines were closed and the operating engines were retired to a siding, from where they were ignominiously tipped into the Sorroe Culebra quarry in the 1930s by employees of the Largo refinery. And there, as far as anyone knows, they remain, buried beneath mounds of garbage, awaiting rediscovery and rescue!

Much of the remaining rail of the Aruba Phosphate Company was lifted, and along with many of the wagons, was moved to the Shell Oil Refinery in Curaçao. Eventually, apart from the loading pier, little evidence remained of the Aruba Phosphate Company and its once busy steam-operated narrow gauge mineral railway.

Refinery railways

The harbour at Sint Nicolaas had a re-birth in 1924 when an oil transhipment facility was built by the Largo Petroleum Company (later to become the Largo Oil & Transportation Co. Ltd). The remaining Aruba Phosphate Company rails were in use again as gasoline-powered 4wPM Milwaukee locos hauled flat cars laden with the pipe and other materials needed to build the transhipment facility.

By 1927 a decision was made to refine the oil at Sint Nicolaas, rather than transport it to Curaçao for refining. The refinery was to be built in the area of the defunct phosphate mines, and once again the matter of the change in elevation between the pier and the flat land above became a problem, as loads needed to be hauled up the grade from the harbour, rather than taken down the grade, as was the case with the loaded phosphate trains.

The problem was resolved by adding a third rail to the 30 inch line to make it standard gauge. A number of standard gauge 100-ton flat cars were brought in to replace the 10-ton narrow gauge cars, and two narrow gauge Milwaukee locomotives often struggled up the hill with laden standard gauge flat cars. One locomotive would be in front hauling and the other would be at the rear acting as a pusher. At times even a winch was used in order to assist the two diminutive locomotives with their outsize loads! With the completion of the construction phase in 1929, the standard gauge line was removed and the system returned to its previous narrow gauge operation.

The refinery-operated Pan American Railroad in Aruba laid a third rail to facilitate the use of standard gauge locomotives for hauling narrow gauge cars. (Carol Burns)

Eventually a new pier was constructed, supplied with new heavier 45 lb steel rail, and the original Plymouth's were replaced with 11 Brookville, 6-ton, 4wPM locomotives. By the end of hostilities in 1946, the locomotive fleet was worn out, and an order was placed for four, 10-ton, diesel-powered locomotives from the same builder.

The limitations of a fixed transport system told against the railway, and with road trucks becoming more easily obtainable after the Second World War, the end for the rail system became inevitable. The last movement on this once extensive rail system took place in November 1985, the refinery closing a year later. Shortly afterwards almost all traces of the refinery and the railway had been removed and the remaining locomotives scrapped. In 1998 a new park was built on the site by the Aruba Government.

The Eagle Railway

Concurrent with the building of the Largo Refinery, the Eagle Refinery was being built on the outskirts of Oranjestad, the main settlement on the island. Aruba, with its convenient location between the oil fields of Venezuela and the industrial might of North America, was a perfect location to undertake oil refining, and the Eagle Petroleum Co., a subsidiary of Shell Oil, constructed a refinery on the island and began refining in 1928. Much of the refinery equipment and construction materials were moved to and around the site by two 2 ft 0 in gauge Muir Hill of England 4wDM locomotives hauling flat cars that were coupled with ridged bars, the length of which could be adjusted to give overhang clearance for the large refinery components being moved.

As at Largo, once construction was completed, the railway became a people and freight mover. The large area covered by refineries meant a lot of walking to and from the canteen, so each day the Eagle railway operated a passenger service between the many work sites throughout the refinery, also moving fresh and frozen foodstuffs from the dock to the commissary area.

Eventually expanding business and larger tanker ships required a new pier to be built to replace the original timber structure, and by 1930 the refinery boasted some five miles of track, including the much longer new pier. However, events in the Second World War saw the elimination of refining at the site, and the railway was inactive for most of this time. Around 1945 a new diesel-engined Hunslet was brought in to replace the two smaller Muir Hills, but the economics of scale defeated the development of additional refining at the site and by 1958 the Hunslet was helping remove the refinery equipment as it was dismantled. The final reminder of the refinery and its little railway came in 1974 when the large pier was removed prior to conversion of the site to a beach resort, as tourism became the new economic force on Aruba.

Curaçao

The Curaçao Mining Company

Curaçao, the largest of the ABC islands, shares a similar geology with Aruba, its neighbour to the west. It was therefore no surprise that in 1874 a vast deposit of high-grade phosphate was discovered in the eastern part of the island near Table Mountain.

Sea access was provided at Fuik Bay, and a tramway and inclined plane were used to transport high-grade phosphate rock to the dock for shipping. The incline used the familiar two-track system, where the weight of the heavily loaded cars was used to haul the empty cars

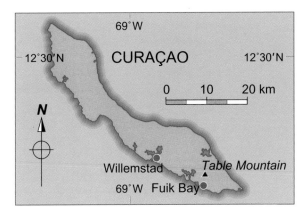

phosphates did not slacken. As car loads increased and the rail system expanded a decision was made to retire the donkeys and invest in locomotives. Water shortage, a perennial problem on the island, ruled out steam locomotives and so a batch of second-hand Plymouth 4wPM locomotives were purchased and put to work. While these locomotives worked well, by the end of the Second World War they were worn out, and an order was placed for four brand new locomotives from Plymouth. Even though ore production had fallen by the late 1950s, a further six additional locomotives were ordered from Plymouth, this time larger 6-ton and 8-ton units. The incline was replaced by conveyor belts in 1960, and only two locomotives and about a mile of railway were in operation by the early 1970s. By the mid-1970s the mine and the railway system had closed completely.

One other railway operated on Curaçao. In 1915 construction began on a refinery owned by Shell Oil. Track and cars salvaged from the defunct Aruba Phosphate Company were pressed into service moving spoil as the site was levelled, and assisting in the movement of equipment and stores. The system was operated by manpower, and no locomotives were ever used.

up the incline for re-filling. Donkeys, the Caribbean, all-purpose power source, were used to haul and spot cars between the various drifts at the mine and haul loaded cars to the top of the incline. After a number of successful years of operation the mine closed in 1887.

As with the Aruba Phosphate Company, by the early part of the twentieth century the market for low-grade agricultural phosphate was being supplied by mines from North America and North Africa. However, Curaçao phosphate, unlike that of Aruba, was of high enough quality to be used in the new steel-making process. In 1910 the mine reopened under new owners as the Mijnmaschappij Curaçao (Curaçao Mining Company), specifically to mine phosphate ore for use in blast furnaces.

The old underground workings were soon abandoned in favour of more efficient surface workings. The internal railway and incline system were strengthened, and a system of light 18 in gauge portable track was used to bring mined material to fixed loading points in preparation for transfer to the dock, via a 30 in gauge tramway. The 6-mile system was, as usual, donkey-powered, using tipping cars supplied by Robert Hudson of Leeds, England.

The 1930s saw the mine weathering the Great Depression, as the demand for steel-making

Plymouth locomotive and Hudson tip wagons from the Curaçao phosphate mine. Preserved at the Curaçao Museum, Willemstad. (Rabbi W.L. Rothschild)

Chapter 13

Guyana and Belize

While Guyana and Belize are not part of the insular Caribbean, the political history and commercial and cultural ties both countries share and continue to develop with the islands of the Caribbean make it fitting that they are included in this book.

GUYANA

Three separate former Dutch possessions were combined in 1831 to form the new South American colony of British Guiana. The country, also once known as Demerara, and now known as the Co-operative Republic of Guyana, is located on the north-east coast of South America. Its vast interior (the country covers about 83,000 square miles) includes large areas of savannah and tropical forest as well as substantial mineral resources. Three big rivers, the Essequibo, Demerara and Berbice, drain the interior of the country and flow to the Atlantic Ocean. Georgetown, the country's capital and main economic centre is situated on the coast at the mouth of the Demerara River.

The Georgetown – Mahaica Railway

The Georgetown to Mahaica Railway was to run along the east coastal plain, a substantial agricultural and sugar cane growing area, and connect Georgetown

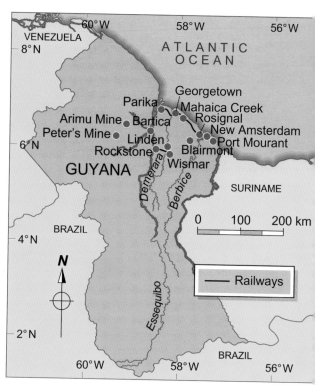

with the Mahaica River. As agricultural produce and the products of the sugar factories were at the time moved laboriously by 'punt' and schooner along the coast to Georgetown, it was felt that a railway would be faster and cheaper, and not subject to the vagaries of wind and tides.

At a general meeting held in Georgetown in March of 1837, the various gentlemen present passed a resolution that '... regarded the speedy and extensive introduction of Iron Railways into British Guiana as of great importance to the interest of the Colony'. The gentlemen were going to need the patience of a saint as it turned out, as the railway took 19 years and many financial twists and turns until it finally reached its destination, only 21½ miles from its starting point!

Given the initial enthusiasm, a joint stock company was soon put in place and almost 2000 £50 shares were to be issued. However, this initial enthusiasm seemed to have died quickly, and nothing further is heard of the Georgetown-Mahaica Railway.

The Demerara Railway Company

It was not until 1845 that the subject of a railway between Georgetown and Mahaica was broached again, this time with more success. Money for construction of the standard gauge line, to be known as the Demerara or East Coast Railway, was to be raised not only locally but also in Great Britain, a decision that, while expedient at the time, later caused all sorts of problems for the owners and operators of the railway. As often happened with Caribbean railways (and railways elsewhere) the project was made more attractive to investors by providing conservative construction estimates, prompted in part by the fact that no tunnels were required, and optimistic freight volume projections.

It was evident that a resident engineer was required and a Mr F. Catherwood accepted the post, arriving in the colony in 1845. Catherwood's initial survey report is thorough and wide ranging; he even suggested that the local peat or 'pegass' could be harvested and dried for use as a locomotive fuel – a suggestion never acted upon. Another Catherwood suggestion was that the line should be elevated through most of the coastal estates through which it passed, allowing strategically-placed bridges to be used to facilitate the movement of field traffic. However, he was overruled by the local directors and his unsuccessful appeal to the directors in England was a foretaste of what was soon to turn into a local versus overseas battle between the two groups, often with the unfortunate Mr Catherwood stuck in the middle.

By all accounts he had somewhat of a predilection for getting himself in the middle of the two factions anyway. When the ceremonial spade and wheelbarrow ordered from England for the first sod turning in August of 1847 did not arrive on time, the Chief Engineer defied the local management committee (who wanted to keep the affair a quiet one) and invited numerous guests, much to the chagrin of many others who were excluded!

Given the circumstances of his employment, Mr Catherwood would need a sense of humour and this was in evidence when the first of the line's English-built locomotives arrived, as they were named *The Mosquito*, *The Sandfly* and *The Firefly*. Two subsequent locomotives were named *The Centipede* and *The Scorpion!*

Work on the line continued in rather a desultory fashion, a shortage of labour and money seemingly the greatest hindrances to progress, and it was not until late in 1847 that four miles of track had been laid. The railway suffered the first of a number of accidents in January of 1848 when a director's inspection train was derailed by a wandering cow and two ejected passengers were fatally injured after being run over by the locomotive. By November of 1848 the line was in operation as far as Plaisance, just six miles from Georgetown. No ceremonial opening this time, just the introduction of two outward and two inward bound trains each day that quickly developed a substantial

Railway travel at its most delightful. One of the Sharp Stewart locomotives and a 4-wheel passenger carriage of the Demerara Railway Company, photographed at Mahaica Creek, 17 August, 1898. (Royal Commonwealth Society Collection, Cambridge University Library)

passenger traffic. Incidentally, this was the first railway to begin operation in South America.

Local Government loans had to be resorted to by 1850 in order to continue progress, and despite the continuing acrimony between the local and overseas director, the line was extended an additional four miles or so to Buxton and then onwards to Enmore and Belfield. The local management committee was dissolved by the overseas directors and the new Resident Engineer also became the railway's General Manager. His proposal to lease the line was rejected, and by 1852 the local press was beginning to take pot shots at the line, reporting that one train took over four hours to travel eight miles and only made it that far by being pushed by a gang of men!

By 1854 there was some improvement in the railway's affairs with the local paper reporting that a 36-truck train, estimated to weigh 300 tons, left Georgetown under the power of one engine. The

transport benefits long promised by the railway were beginning to become a reality. Additional work extended the line another two miles east and things seemed to be going well, when news was received in the colony that the rejected proposal to lease the line had now been accepted and Mr Manifold, the former Resident Engineer, Manager and then Lessee, was about to return and complete the line to Mahaica from which point in time he could take over and operate the railway. Considering the amount of money the Colonial Government had pumped into the railway, this did not sit at all well with the local community and shareholders.

More financial machinations and daily operational problems left estate owners along the line without the means of shipping their produce to Georgetown, as by now most of the coastal sailing vessels had been abandoned, resulting in considerable hardship. By 1858 passenger services were drastically reduced and the Colonial Government was forced out of necessity to import goods wagons for the sake of the estate owners along the line. Two new locomotives were delivered in 1859 in an attempt to revitalise the service, but to little avail. A contemporary article in the colony's leading newspaper, stated that 'We would not wish our worst enemy greater evil than to be made the sole proprietor of the Demerara Railway Company...'

However, by 1864 things were definitely on the mend. Two new locomotives, the *Alexandra* and *Victoria*, had arrived from Sharp Stewart in England, and a further extension of the line had been laid to Clonbrook. A dividend and interest on share stock was paid, and in August 1864 a party of invited guests positively romped along from Georgetown to the new terminus at Mahaica, a distance of $21\frac{1}{2}$ miles, in just over 90 minutes. There were no fatalities on this occasion. The line had taken 18 years to build and had cost £313,890, an astronomical figure by any measure for 20 miles of single track, standard gauge tunnel-less railway.

The East Coast Railway began to enjoy a period of relatively trouble-free operation and although the company was reluctant to participate in any extension of the line, just when it was turning a profit, in 1897 they were prevailed upon to construct a further 39 miles of track to Rosignol on the Berbice River on what was often known as the 'Berbice Extension'. The 61½-mile east coast line now connected Georgetown with New Amsterdam, the colony's second largest city, just across the river from Rosignol.

The 3ft 6in gauge West Coast Railway was built at the same time westwards to connect Vreed-en-Hoop (across the Demerara River from Georgetown) with Greenwich Park, a distance of 15 miles. An additional

▲ *Built c.1864 by Sharp Stewart, Alexandra was reportedly still providing sterling service on the British Guiana Railway in 1924. (Royal Commonwealth Society Collection, University of Cambridge Library)*

◀ Sir Graeme *was one of two new engines ordered from Great Britain in 1924 for the British Guiana Railway. (Royal Commonwealth Society Collection, University of Cambridge Library)*

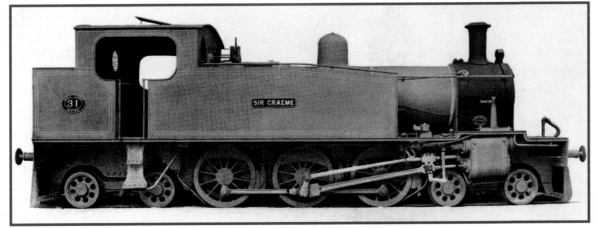

3½ miles laid in 1914 took the line further west to Parika. The lack of success of these two extensions was partly the cause of the Government takeover of the coastal railways.

In Government hands

In 1918 the Colonial Government appointed a committee to investigate the operation of the railway, this step being instigated in large part by public dissatisfaction with the service being offered. Part of the mandate of the Commission was to advise the colony on the possible 'nationalisation' of the railway. In a move that seemed almost inevitable, the east and west coast lines were acquired by the Colonial Government's transport department in January 1922.

Once under control of the Colonial Transportation Department, which incidentally operated a fleet of ferry and coastal steamers, there was considerable investment in the railway. On acquisition, the railway had a fleet of 16 locomotives, the two oldest were probably the *Alexandra* and *Victoria* dating from 1863, the most recent one dating from 1921. Two new passenger locomotives were introduced in 1924, both handsome 4-6-4 tank engines, in order to augment this fleet of older and basically worn-out locomotives, and a number of passenger coaches were rebuilt. Permanent way repairs were instituted and the railway entered a period of growth and stability.

In 1943 the annual report of the railway referred to the problems of operating a colonial railway during war time. New boilers that had been ordered for older locomotives prior to the start of the war had not yet arrived, fuel and parts were hard to come by and passenger services had to be curtailed in order to conserve scarce resources. Two ex-United States War department petrol locomotives and some wagons had been obtained to help augment the railways rolling stock. The acquisition of the entire locomotive fleet, rolling stock and anything else removable from the closed Bermuda Railway in 1948 helped the line, now known as the Demerara Railway, provide the level of service required. As the Bermuda equipment was standard gauge, it could only be utilised between Georgetown and Rosignol, but this was enough to turn the railway around. In 1953 almost 1¼ million passengers and over 90,000 tons of freight were carried. While it had been a long wait, the potential envisioned by the line's original promoters had become reality.

As fate would have it, however, the ex-Bermuda Railway equipment was again faced with competition from road transport, and as a more substantial highway network developed in Guyana the east-coast railway, begun with such hope in 1838, could not compete. Along with the west-coast line it was eventually closed in 1972. This time there was no reprieve for the Bermuda Railway equipment and it was scrapped, along with the locomotives and rolling stock of the Demerara Railway.

Rails in the interior

Guyana is a large country, about the same size as Idaho and has an interior rich in mineral and timber. In 1897 a metre-gauge railway was opened in the interior to connect Wismar, on the right bank of the Demarara River (about 65 miles from its mouth at Georgetown) with Rockstone on the right bank of the Essequibo River. The incentive for the construction of this line was the desire to make the new Potaro goldfields more accessible, as the river route along the Essequibo was hampered by a number of falls. The line was a private venture, built by Sprotson's Dock and Foundry Co, a Georgetown company that had considerable interest in the interior of the country as well as operating a number of ferries into the interior from the coast. The line, 18¾ miles long, was built with the assistance of an interest-free loan from the Colonial Government. Running through extensive tropical hardwood forests, the railway encouraged the development of a substantial logging industry in the area.

In the 1920s the line had five locomotives and 31 flat cars, many of which would have been adapted to carry large hardwood logs to the river for transhipment to the coast. This was another railway lost to a developing road system and cheap trucks.

Mineral and sugar railways

Bauxite is found in considerable quantity in the interior of Guyana and sugar cane cultivation and processing, while not on the same scale as many of the Caribbean islands, has always been an important agricultural industry in the country, especially along the flat, coastal plains.

There were only two sugar Central railways in Guyana. These were at Blairmont plantation, to the south of Rosignol, and at the Port Mourant plantation, on the coast just east of New Amsterdam. The former estate used two 7-ton petrol locomotives made in the United States on a 4-mile-long system and the latter used two, 12-ton Fowler locomotives from England on a 5-mile long, light rail system. Cane workers were transported on this system in open-sided passenger cars also built by Fowlers. Many other sugar Centrals shipped cane from the fields to the factory by means of animal-drawn steel barges. As most of the cane land was below sea level an extensive system of drainage canals was established (much like Holland) and so these provided a ready and less costly means of transport than a railway.

Large bauxite resources are found in the area of Linden, the second largest town in the country, 70 miles south of Georgetown. The Demba railway operated in the bauxite mine, and the Manganese Railway performed a similar duty for the Manganese Mining Company. Open-cast mines now use trucks and barges to transport the ore, replacing the narrow gauge railways previously used.

BELIZE

Belize, formerly British Honduras, was originally settled in the late 1600s by English loggers, attracted to the country by vast stands of tropical hardwoods. Although only about one-tenth of the area of Guyana,

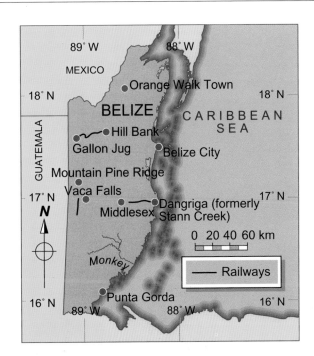

Belize has a similar environment and economy. The interior of the country is wet and despite extensive logging remains heavily forested. Agriculture plays a large part in the economy of the country, and as in Guyana, most of the population lives along the flat coastal areas.

The Stann Creek Railway

Until the development of short railway lines in the interior of British Honduras, transportation was usually along bush trails or rivers. Loggers in the interior traditionally used small boats on the country's extensive network of rivers to reach areas where trees could be cut, and used the same rivers to float cut logs to the coast, where they could be loaded for export. When human labour was used to move the logs to water, logging operations could only take place on the banks of the rivers. The introduction of oxen in the early 1800s allowed loggers to venture up to 10 miles

107

into the forest. However, by the latter part of the 1800s it was obvious that a railway would facilitate the harvesting of lumber far from water sources, thus expanding the timber trade of the colony.

Plans for a railway into the interior attracted a lot of local attention in the 1880s, but the actual establishment of a railway was tied in with very complex diplomatic dealings with Guatemala, Belize's neighbour to the south and west. The several railways

Bananas were always a large part of the traffic on the Stann Creek Railway. The locomotive and banana cars shown here will have been to the end of the pier at Commerce Bight to unload into the ship. (Belize Archives Dept)

proposed were much more extensive than those eventually built, and were designed to tap the interior of the country for both timber and agriculture, as well as being part of a grandiose trans-continental railway linking North and South America and the Atlantic and Pacific Oceans. Eventually, it was an outside catalyst that helped precipitate the building of the colony's main public line, the Stann Creek Railway.

In 1892 the current Governor of the colony officially opened a privately-owned light railway from Stann Creek (now known as Dangriga) to Melinda, a distance a little over five miles north-west from the coast, the railway being used to transport fruit being grown in the district. The railway had been built by the British Honduras Syndicate, a private company

working to develop the fruit-growing industry in that area. The line was eventually extended to Middlesex, and while not considered by locals or the Colonial Office in England to be the answer to the colony's railway requirements, it was successful in helping to promote fruit and agriculture in the areas through which it ran.

Eventually, the Colonial Government was convinced of the need to build a railway, and a route for the Stann Creek Railway was surveyed through the Stann Creek Valley running south of Stann Creek Town to the Melinda tramway. Construction began in 1907, and a year later the first section was open to traffic. Work was completed on the whole section by 1914. The Stann Creek Railway extended 25 miles, from the railway pier at Commerce Bight to Middlesex in the interior, passing through the rich alluvial soils of the Stann Creek Valley. The British Honduras banana industry began as part of the Central American banana boom of the late 1800s, and it was hoped that the railway would generate most of its revenue from the transport of this fruit from the interior to the deep-water pier.

The original plans called for a light railway of only 20 in gauge, but this idea was quickly changed due to pressure from the local Legislature and a 3 ft 0 in gauge line, laid with 40 lb rail, was eventually constructed. The line was an easy one, with a maximum grade of 1 in 65. Steel bridges, steel spans and concrete abutments were employed along the line to provide some protection from the large amounts of flood water often encountered. Much of the construction work was carried out by labourers from Caribbean islands, especially Jamaica. The pier at Commerce Bight had between 21 and 24 ft of water at all times, allowing the use of large ocean-going vessels. Railway headquarters and the station were located a few miles north of Commerce Bight pier, and about one and a half miles south of Stann Creek Town. Living quarters for management staff, engine houses, offices, storerooms and employee housing were all located here, in what turned out to be a very bad mosquito area that often saw railway staff laid up with malaria.

By 1925 railway activity was much reduced due to the ravages of 'Panama Disease' in the fledgling banana industry. The Railway Superintendent's annual reports throughout the 1920s invariably mentioned dwindling revenues and the steps being taken to effect economy measures on the railway.

However, the railway was still able to operate two trains per week. Monday's train was a work train which left the station by Stann Creek Town at 6.30 am and made its way into the interior, dropping off work gangs, freight and supplies as needed. The train would then return to Stann Creek pushing the cars ahead, a practice which lead to the line's only fatal accident when an old lady, using the right of way as a path, was struck and killed by the lead wagon. On Thursdays a train went out into the country in the early morning to collect bananas and other agricultural produce that had been harvested that week by the work gangs. Loaded cars were shunted onto the pier of Commerce Bight for loading into United Fruit Company steamers.

In 1921 the line carried 4628 tons of freight and 4166 passengers over 25 miles of track, using four small, English-built, tank locomotives, two passenger cars and over 40 fruit cars for the carriage of bananas. The reality was that there was little opportunity to increase traffic, and by 1923 the Acting Superintendent of Railways was reporting to the Governor of the colony that unless the Government was prepared to keep operating the railway at a substantial loss, something was going to have to be done in the near future.

In 1925 an agreement was reached between the Government of British Honduras and the American-owned Tidewater Lumber Co. to use the line for carrying lumber from Middlesex to the pier for export to the United States, providing a boost in the line's fortunes. In early 1933 light motor passenger cars were introduced and fares were cut drastically, and for a

The Tidewater Lumber Co transporting mahogany destined for foreign markets. (Author's collection)

short period this service showed a profit. However, it was not sufficient to reverse the fortunes of the Stann Creek Railway and the line finally closed in 1937. Road building in the colony began in earnest in the 1930s, with roads connecting Belize City with Corozol, Orange Walk and Cayo, while the Western Highway extended as far as Stann Creek. In a bitter-sweet move, the line of the defunct Stann Creek Railway was converted to a highway in 1939-40, the original railway bridges often being incorporated into the new highway.

Logging railways

Belize has a climate that provides ideal growing conditions for tropical hardwoods such as mahogany, as well as pines. Harvesting of mahogany trees is best done in winter after the rainy season, and as timber

This 18-ton, two-truck Shay, built in 1925, would have been ideal for use on the rough tracks of the Mengel Co.'s British Honduras timber-haulage railway. (Allen County Historical Society, Lima, Ohio)

cutting moved further and further away from the river banks logging railways or tramways were to become the most efficient means of moving the harvested trees to points on one of the many rivers that run though the interior, where they could be put into the water to float to the coast for processing or export. A number of logging railways were developed in the interior of Belize, although none remain today.

The Mengel Company of Kentucky began logging in Belize in 1925-6, establishing a narrow gauge railway in the area of the Vaca Falls. The falls prevented logs being floated down-river, as was the normal practice, so a 15-mile single line was laid from loading points in the area of Mountain Pine Ridge to the river below the Falls. American logging practice saw cut logs hauled to the rail line by strategically placed steam winches, and then loaded onto flat cars and hauled to drop-off points on the river by one of the

two Shay locomotives used on the railway. The line ran for the last time in 1952.

The Gliksten Group from England built a logging railway in the north-western region of Belize running from the logging village of Gallon Jug, near the Guatemalan border, to the village of Hill Bank, a distance of about 25 miles. The narrow gauge railway was built during the period 1890-1930 and had closed in or by 1956. A number of wheel sets and flat cars were taken from the abandoned railway to the extensive Belize City lumber yards owned by Gliksten, where they were used on a man-powered railway.

From Gallon Jug (it got its name from three old gallon jugs found at the site when originally cleared in the 1940s) logs were transported by rail to Hill Bank and from there floated to Orange Walk Town and then to Belize City. In later years a diesel locomotive was used to haul the logging train and a 4-wheeled motor bus was used for passenger runs between Gallon Jug, which was the terminus for the railway, and Hill Bank.

The Victoria Falls Co. operated a short logging railway in the northern part of the country, as did Belize Estate & Produce Co. They were both loggers and fruit growers. The latter operated a short logging railway in the same area.

Banana tramways

Two tramways, one owned by the British Honduras Syndicate running about eight miles inland from Stann Creek to just past Melinda, and the other connecting the Sennis and Monkey River, in the south, were used to transport bananas to the coast for export. A dock at Punta Gorda, near the southern border with Guatemala, had a rail facility, as a postcard shows banana cars on the dock there, but little other information is known.

Chapter 14

Street railways

Urban expansion and industrialisation came at the same time to many of the larger Caribbean islands. Post-emancipation migration from sugar plantations swelled the populations of cities and urban centres, and by the late 1800s efficient public transport systems became a pressing need in these densely-populated centres. Street railways, initially horse or mule powered, were introduced as a means of transporting large numbers of commuting workers to and from the ever expanding downtown or city centres.

Street railway equipment manufacturers in North America, Britain and Europe were soon competing to supply the infrastructure needed to operate these systems. The introduction of electricity, often provided by generating stations owned by foreign investors, provided a more efficient alternative to animal power, and by the early 1900s a number of towns and cities in the Caribbean had extensive, modern, street railways. Their demise, in common with the public railways on these islands, was brought about by the adoption of buses, cars and taxis.

Cuba

Cuba had the Caribbean's first street railway, a short system introduced to the streets of Havana in 1858, using horse-drawn, American-built trams. These were replaced by a much more extensive standard gauge electric street railway that began operation in 1901 with a stable of over 100 single-truck, American-built cars that collected current from overhead lines via twin poles. The system, owned and operated by the American-owned Havana Electric Railway was obviously well patronised as it subsequently operated a fleet of over 500 cars! In 1924 a magazine advertisement for the Hotel Plaza in downtown Havana noted that the golf course at the Havana Country Club was only 35 minutes away by the electric cars that passed the hotel door, and the new sub-division at Mirimar, a suburb to the east of the capital 'had been fostered to a large extent by the new car lines being built. Nationalised in 1950, the system ceased operation in early 1952.

A Jackson & Sharp power trolley and trailer of the Havana Electric Railway on palm-lined Cerro Street, in downtown Havana. (Author's collection)

A Brill car of the Compania Electrica de Santiago passing the Parque Aguilera in downtown Santiago de Cuba, Cuba. (Author's collection)

The Constant Spring tramcar passing the Supreme Court building on King Street in downtown Kingston, Jamaica. (National Library of Jamaica)

Four-wheel, open-ended Brill cars provided services on the electric street railway operating in Santiago de Cuba in 1908. The system was brought out by the Havana Electric Railway in 1926 and ceased operations in 1952. Beginning in the early 1900s there was considerable Canadian investment in utilities and transportation systems in both the Caribbean and Central and South America, and the Canadian-owned street railway in the city of Camagüey began operating in 1908. Eventually equipped with Brill cars, it was purchased by Havana Electric in 1926 and closed in 1952. East of Havana, the city of Matanzas began with a battery-powered street railway in 1916 but later changed to a wire and power pole operation that lasted

until closing in 1954. Other short battery-powered street railways ran in the towns of Cienfuegos and Cardenas from 1915 to the mid-1920s.

Jamaica

Trams disappeared from the streets of Kingston, the large and busy capital of Jamaica, in 1948 after a period of 72 years. In 1862 a tramway act was passed by the Jamaican Government, but it was not until 1876 that the first tramway was opened in the capital. Kingston had replaced Spanish Town as the island's capital in 1872, and by 1876 substantial urbanisation was taking place around the new capital. It was hoped that a street railway would encourage further suburban development and help relieve inner-city overcrowding.

The Jamaica Street Car Company began by using mules as power. While most services operated in the downtown district, the longest ride was out to Constant Spring, to the north of the city. Passenger numbers increased to well over one million by 1896, making the use of mule-power slow and expensive. It was time to improve and electrify the system.

The West India Electric Company Limited (Canada) became the new owners of the street railway in 1897, and while a completely new electric-powered system was installed, continued to operate mule-powered trams until 1907 when they acquired the Jamaica Electric Light and Power Company. The electric line opened for operation in March of 1899, using current generated by a hydro-electric station on the Rio Cobre river to the north-west of Kingston. The service was extended and new Canadian-built cars were introduced. Despite a violent earthquake in 1910 that demolished trams and company buildings, progress on the tramway continued. However, what the earthquake could not stop, public demonstrations against fare increases and employee strikes could and in 1923 the West India Electric Company transferred the remainder of its operating lease to another Canadian company, the Jamaica Public Service Company Limited (JPSCo). The Kingston street railway system eventually extended over a length of 25 miles, only being reduced on the advent of competing bus services when less remunerative routes were abandoned in favour of a more central system. Competition from motor buses began after the First World War, and as the JPSCo had no exclusive licence to provide commuter services in the city, the omnibuses finally proved to be the demise of the Kingston tramway system in 1948.

Hispaniola

In Port-au-Prince, Haiti, a horse-powered street railway opened in 1878. The horses were replaced by a steam-powered system in 1897, with the 2 ft 6 in gauge system using American Porter locomotives hauling 'toast-rack' type cars. The locomotives were of 0-4-2 wheel arrangement and were properly designed for use on street railways, with covered motion work and wheels and a clerestory roof to aid ventilation on the footplate. The system was never electrified, and it is not known when it finally closed, but a very poor photograph shows what appears to be a motor truck converted to a passenger car running on rails in front of the American Embassy in Port-au-Prince.

In the early 1900s several animal-powered street railway or tramway systems were operating in the Dominican Republic's capital Santo Domingo, Puerto Plata on the north coast and in Montecristi further west on the coast by the Yaque del Norte. These systems were never electrified and seem to have had a short operating life.

Taken sometime between 1897 and 1932 on the Port-au-Prince, Haiti, street railway. This view shows Assuel, an 0-4-2 tank engine built by Krauss of Germany, with a rake of American-built passenger cars. (Geoffrey Hill collection)

Puerto Rico

Puerto Rico's first railway venture was in 1872, when a street car railway was laid in the west-coast town of Mayagüez, using English-built cars. A contemporary photograph shows what appears to be a 4-wheel, narrow gauge, single deck, open car being pulled by a horse and a mule harnessed in tandem (a quite common combination). While the Mayagüez system was operated by battery power in the First World War period, it was not as extensive as that developed for the island's capital, San Juan.

After the United States occupation of Puerto Rico in 1898, considerable American investment was made in the island's transportation infrastructure. In 1901 a standard gauge combination electric street car and urban railway system was instituted between downtown San Juan (the area now called 'Old San Juan') and the evolving suburbs of Santurce and Rio Piedras to the south. As also happened in Havana, the electric railway was obviously an asset to the new development and it was reported soon after its opening that Rio Piedras was now home to many wealthy San Juan businessmen. Both areas are now part of the urban conurbation of the new San Juan, and it is hard to believe that in the early part of this century these new settlements were out in the country. The line

opened using substantial American-built, twin bogie cars, these not being replaced until the 1920s by more modern single-end cars. The service was withdrawn in 1946.

Ponce is a large town on the south coast of Puerto Rico and electric-powered Brill cars replaced ones powered by animals on the town's metre-gauge street railway in 1902. The system was an early victim to closure, ending services in 1927.

Martinique

Saint-Pierre, located on the north-west coast of Martinique, was a town of considerable size and wealth by the late 1800s. With a wealth created by the many sugar factories and rum distilleries in the surrounding countryside, the town was an important and busy port that boasted substantial municipal buildings, an opera house and some of the most fashionable shops in the French West Indies. A horse-powered street railway ran the length of the town's waterfront main street, more as a fashion statement than an essential transport system. Saint-Pierre well deserved its sobriquet 'the Paris of the Caribbean'. However, all this wealth and glamour, along with the town's 30,000 inhabitants and the street railway, disappeared in an instant at 7.50 am on 8 May, 1902, when the nearby volcano, Mt Pelée, exploded and enveloped the town in super-heated gases and pyroclastic flow. While the town was eventually rebuilt, the street railway, like the opera house, remains only a memory.

Barbados

A horse-powered street railway began operating in

▲ *Postmarked 1926, this card was mailed a year after the Bridgetown Tramway closed. Two cars pass by the seaside park at Hastings Rock. (Author's collection)*

▶ *Trafalgar Square, the centre of Bridgetown, Barbados, was the terminus for the Bridgetown Tramway Co. Five of the company's 20 cars are in this photograph. (Author's collection)*

Bridgetown, the capital of Barbados, in 1885. By the mid-1850s Barbados was already a densely-populated island and a Government committee had been established in 1851 to report on a citizens' petition for the establishment of a publicly-owned inter-urban tramway system that would extend beyond the confines of Bridgetown. While the committee reported favourably on the concept, they felt the estimated cost of between £4000 and £5000 per mile was far too much for the island Government to bear.

In 1882, a year after the Barbados Railway began operation, the idea of a tramway was revived, but to serve only Bridgetown. This time the proposal was not only approved, but financial backing was found on Barbados, and the Barbados Tramway Company began operating in 1885 when the first section from Bridgetown east to Hastings Rock was opened. A month later the route west to Fontabelle was opened. By 1905 the street railway had nine miles of track, and 20 horse-drawn, open-sided, 4-wheel cars operating five routes. The hub of the system was in Trafalgar

Square, a central spot in Bridgetown by the side of the Constitution River and the Parliament Building. That same year a small news item appeared in the local newspaper noting the proposal for a motor omnibus service that had been put forward by a local businessman. The article noted prophetically that, if accepted, the proposal would be a serious blow to the 'light railway' (it is not clear whether this was the street railway, or the Barbados Railway), and it would put out of business the old-fashioned (horse-drawn) omnibus' that ran between Bridgetown and Speightstown, just up the coast.

In 1910 the company was sold to American interests and plans were made to extend rails south to Oistins and northwards into St Jame's parish, both heavily-populated areas. The extensions were never built and the tramway, using horse-power till the end, closed in July 1925, the victim of competition from the more flexible and speedier buses that eventually appeared on the streets of Bridgetown.

Trinidad

Port of Spain, the capital of Trinidad, is now a bustling city of substantial size located on the Gulf of Paria. In 1808 a disastrous fire swept through the old town and little survived. The opportunity was taken to lay out a new town on the same site, but this time with wide streets and avenues, a plan later to be perfect for the introduction of a street railway! The population of the city grew considerably after emancipation in 1834, and by the late 1870s the city had sufficient population to warrant the introduction of a street railway.

In 1879 a Mr Roblins of New York City asked for a concession to operate a street railway; the ordinance being issued in 1882. By the following year work had begun on laying a 3 ft 6 in gauge, mule-powered system that would run from the main railway station downtown to Cipriani Boulevard via Tragarete Road. This line was later extended to Corcorite. Additional street railway services were offered by the Belmont Tramway Company system that headed north from the centre of town to Belmont, just south of Queen's Park Savannah. Opened in 1895, this was the first electric-powered railway in the West Indies, pre-dating the Kingston, Jamaica system by four years, and was only the third in Latin America.

Trinidad Electric Light & Power Co. bought the narrow gauge Belmont line in 1900 and rebuilt it as a standard gauge line equipped with Brill cars in 1902, taking over Port-of-Spain's other street railway a year

▼ The St Anns and St Clair trams on Frederick Street, Port-au-Spain, Trinidad, sometime during the mid-1920s. The system used a fleet of Brill cars. (Royal Commonwealth Society Collection, Cambridge Univeristy Library)

later. Eventually the combined system used 45-seater, open-sided, single-pole cars with clerestory roofs. The junction of all routes was at Frederick Street and Marine Square, where the east-west and north-south lines crossed. A 15-minute service ran from the railway station west to Four Roads, from the railway station north to Belmont, from the railway station to St Clair via Queen's Park and the Maraval corner, and a belt route ran around Queen's Park. The Port of Spain street railway closed in 1950. Motor buses now run from the former main railway station that was also the street railway terminus.

Curaçao

Willemstad, the main town in Curaçao, quickly gained prominence as a port, expanding by the 1880s down both sides of the St Anna Bay. Bridges and ferries joined the divided city, but the problem of transporting commuters into town from the new suburbs became a persistent problem. In 1886 the Curaçao Tramway Company obtained a charter to establish a horse-powered street railway along a one mile route that would terminate in the commercial district. While the railway was an undoubted success, revenues were low and the original owners sold out in 1893, the new owners continuing the horse-drawn service. A second, short-lived line opened in 1896, offering an alternate route. It closed after only seven months of operation.

As Willemstad continued to prosper it became evident that the tiny and slow single horse-drawn street cars were no longer capable of providing an adequate service. In 1904 plans were made to upgrade the system and provide motor-powered cars. By this time the Government had taken an interest in the street railway and, as a condition of granting the operating company a new charter, stipulated that the gauge of

the track be increased to no less than 75 cm (2 ft 6 in), and that conductors must be carried on all cars.

The owner declined to carry out the required improvements and prevaricated over the Government's request for him to adopt the new operating policies. When the Government's patience ran out, his lease was cancelled and a new company, the Curaçao Tramway Service, was awarded the concession. By 1911 a completely new metre-gauge line had been completed, incorporating both the original route and that of the short-lived line of 1896. To replace the obsolete horse cars, three state-of-the-art, 4-wheel motor cars were delivered from the builders, Sidney Strakers & Squire, Ltd. of London, England. The substantial chassis of these cars had been built by the United Electric Co. and were each fitted with a 32-brake horsepower, 4-cylinder, petrol engine. The Double-ended, the cars could accommodate 35 passengers and were geared for 5, 10 and 15 mph speeds, a far cry from the horse trams that were often so overloaded that the poor horse could barely move them. Provision had been made for the hot, dry climate found in Curaçao by the fitting of an external radiator and an engine-driven cooling fan. By all accounts the cars worked well and provided a reliable service during the next ten years.

By the end of the First World War the cars were suffering from a lack of replacement parts, being worn to the point where they were unusable. As no new parts were forthcoming, the operators of the street railway were granted a charter to begin a motor bus service in 1920, signalling the end of the Curaçao street railway. The track was removed shortly after the closure and the cars were shipped to an unknown destination in Venezuela.

Guyana

A horse-powered street railway began operating in the Guyana capital of Georgetown in 1880. It was converted to a standard gauge electric system in 1901 using cars from the United States. Owned at the time of closure by the Demerara Electric Company, the system ceased operation in 1930, one of the first to go in South America.

A fine bird's-eye view of Georgetown, Demerara (now Guyana) with one of the Demerara Electric Company's standard gauge cars in the foreground. (Author's collection)

121

Sources and Bibliography

Many documents, gleaned from a variety of sources, in many locations, have contributed to the writing of this book. Not all the sources used to locate reference material are listed, however those found most productive or accessible are. It should be noted that in the case of Cuba, substantial reference sources are included in *Sugar and Railroads A Cuban History 1837-1959*.

Sources of railway material

Archives located within the Caribbean:

Antigua and Barbuda Museum, St John's, Antigua

Barbados Museum and Historical Society, The Garrison, St Michael, Barbados

Barbados National Trust, St Michael, Barbados

Belize National Archives, Belmopan, Belize

Department of Archives, Nassau, Bahamas

Kitchen Collection, Bermuda Archives, Hamilton, Bermuda

Library and Archives, San Juan, Puerto Rico

National Archives of Trinidad and Tobago, Port of Spain, Trinidad

National Library of Jamaica, Kingston, Jamaica

St Croix Landmarks Society, Whim Museum, St Croix

St Christopher Heritage Society, Basseterre, St Kitts.

Archives located in Great Britain:

Leeds Industrial Museum, Armley Mills, Leeds, England

Mitchell Library, Glasgow, Scotland

Royal Commonwealth Society Collection, Cambridge University Library, Cambridge, England

Rural History Centre, University of Reading, Reading, England

Archives located in the United States:

Allen County Historical Society, Lima, Ohio

Cuba Heritage Collection, Otto G. Richter Library, University of Miami, Maimi, Florida

DeGolyer Library, Southern Methodist University, Dallas, Texas

Railroad Museum of Pennsylvania, Strasburg, Pennsylvania

ALCO Historic Photos, Mowhawk and Hudson Chapter, National Railway Historical Society

Select bibliography

Long, W.R., *Railways of Central America and the West Indies* 'Washington' 1925.

A fascinating document issued by the US Bureau of Foreign and Domestic Commerce in 1925. Author W. Rodney Long was a member of the Transportation Division, and his report covers both public and private railways. While often short on the technical details of locomotives, it nevertheless provides a valuable potted history and operating perspective on many Caribbean railways. Copies of this report are to be found in the Library of Congress, Washington, DC (photocopies can be obtained from the Library Duplication Service), the New York Library and the Royal Commonwealth Society Collection, University of Cambridge Library, England.

Parry, J.H., Sherlock, P. and Manigot, A., *A Short History of the West Indies*, London: Macmillan, 1987.

Ransome, P.J.G., *Narrow Gauge Steam, Its origins and world-wide development*, Somerset: Oxford Publishing Co., 1996.

Robertson, L. S., *Narrow Gauge Railways – Two Feet and Under*, Croydon: Plateway Press, 1988.

Islands and railways

Bahamas

Albury, P., *The Story of the Bahamas*, London: Macmillan, 1975.

Bermuda

Pomeroy, C.A., *The Bermuda Railway Gone-But Not Forgotten*, Bermuda: 1993.

Raine. D. F., *'Rattle and Shake' The Story of the Bermuda Railway*, Bermuda: Pompano Publications, 1994.

Cuba

Cuba Commercial and Financial Magazine,
New York: E. N. Robaina, 1924.

Garcia, A., Zanetti, O., *Caminos para el Azucar,*
Havana: Ciencias Sociales, 1987.

—, *Sugar and Railroads. A Cuban History,
1837-1959,* Chapel Hill: The University of
North Carolina Press, 1998.

Eatwell, D., *Today's Steam on the Sugar lines of
Cuba (Vol. One),* Calgary: British Railway
Modellers of North America, 1998.

Leach, G. A. P., *Industrial Steam Locomotives
of Cuba,* London: Industrial Railway Society,
1996.

Serrano, V., *Cronicas Del Primer Ferrocarril De
Cuba,* Havana: Departmento de
Orientacion, 1973.

Wolf, A.H., *Trains of Cuba, Steam, Diesel and
Electric,* Skookumchuck: Canadian Caboose
Press, 1996.

Guyana

Bayley, S. H., *Railways in British Guiana,*
Georgetown: Government of British Guiana,
1926.

Puerto Rico

Delano. J., *From San Juan to Ponce on the Train,*
Rio Piedra: University of Puerto Rico, 1991.

Locomotives and rolling stock

Alco Historic Photos, Schenectctady: Mohawk and
Hudson Chapter, National Railway
Historical Society, 1984.

Baldwin Locomotive Works Negative Collection,
Strasburg: Railroad Museum of
Pennsylvania, 1989.

Conde, J.C., *Fowler Locomotives in the Kingdom of
Hawaii,* Peterborough: Narrow Gauge
Railway Society, 1993.

Hudson Light Railway Materials, Leeds: Robert
Hudson Ltd., 1957.

Kerr, Stuart's Locomotives, Brighton: Plateway
Press, 1991.

Lima Locomotive Works, Inc. Builders Photographs,
Lima: The Allen County Historical Society,
1988.

Neal, A (ed.), *W.G. Bagnall Ltd. Narrow Gauge
Locomotives and Rolling Stock,* Brighton:
Plateway Press, 1989.

—, *Hunslet Narrow Gauge Locomotives,* Brighton:
Plateway Press, 1995.

Tromp, L. A., *Machinery and Equipment of the
Sugar Cane Factory,* London: Norman
Rogers, 1936.

Street railways

Morrison, A., *Latin America by streetcar.
A Pictorial Survey of Urban Rail Transport
South of the USA,* New York; Bonde Press,
1996.

Journals and periodicals:

Many articles, some general and some specific,
can be found in current and back issues of the
following:

    British Overseas Railway Journal
    Locomotives International
    Railway World
    Railway Magazine
    The Railway Gazette

Organisations

Organisations that are a source of information on
Caribbean railways include:
    The Industrial Railway Society
    The Narrow Gauge Railway Society
    The Industrial Locomotive Society

Web sites

There are an increasing number of web sites
devoted to railways and railway matters. Perusal
of these can sometimes provide historical and
current information related to Caribbean
railways.

Videos

There are currently a few videos available
featuring Caribbean railways. Three that have
been viewed are listed below:

Cuba 1997 – Island Treasures, Canadian Caboose
Press, Skookumchuck, B.C., Canada.

Island Time War – Trains of Cuba, Canadian
Caboose Press.

*The Friendliest Line in the World (The Railways of
Jamaica),* Videolines Ltd., Paddock Wood,
Kent, England.

Index